THE ITALIAN
COLLECTION

Cheese-and-Herb Tortelli Marinara, page 121

THE ITALIAN COLLECTION

American Express Publishing Corporation
New York

FOOD & WINE MAGAZINE
Editor in Chief: Dana Cowin
Food Editor: Tina Ujlaki

FOOD & WINE BOOKS
Editor in Chief: Judith Hill
Production Manager: Yvette Williams-Braxton

Vice President, Books and Information Services: John Stoops
Marketing Director: Mary V. Cooney
Marketing/Promotion Manager: Roni Stein
Operations Manager: Doreen Camardi
Business Manager: David Geller

Wine Consultant: Mary Ewing-Mulligan

Produced by Smallwood & Stewart, Inc., New York City
Editor: Kathy Kingsley
Designer: Liz Trovato
Managing Editor: Deri Reed
Copy Editor: Judith Sutton
Assistant Editor: Stacey Gill
Editorial Consultant: Deborah Mintcheff

Cover Photos: Spaghettini with Uncooked Tomato and Black Olive Sauce, page 82
(front); Ossobuco with Gremolata, page 133, Insalata di Mare, page 33, Ligurian
Vegetable Soup, page 47, Grilled Prosciutto and Fontina Cheese Panini, page 37,
Green Beans with Balsamic-Glazed Onions, page 238, Hazelnut Biscotti with Black
Pepper, page 288 (back)

American Express Publishing Corporation

Library of Congress Catalog Card Number:
The Best of food & wine.   The Italian Collection.
          p.   cm.
                        ISBN 0-916103-36-6
1. Cookery, Italian.   I. Food & wine (New York, N.Y.)   II. Best of food &
wine.   III. Title: Best of food and wine. Italian collection
TX723.B4685   1997
641.5945--dc21
                                                                97-823
                                                                  CIP

Published by American Express Publishing Corporation
1120 Avenue of the Americas, New York, New York, 10036

Manufactured in the United States of America

CONTENTS

Tuscan Roast Loin of Pork, page 155

INTRODUCTION

Most food fanatics, like us, characterize Italian food as simple in method yet superior in flavor. What could be better—great-tasting food that's easy to make. For that very reason, more Italian dishes have run in the magazine over the last few years than recipes from any other country except the United States.

Consider this menu made up of some of our favorites: savory Rosemary-and-Orange Roasted Peppers (page 14) and Rosemary Grissini (page 211); Tagliatelle with Cabbage and Sage (page 89); succulent Tuscan Roast Loin of Pork (page 155) and Braised Mushrooms with Pancetta and Pine Nuts (page 241); and Raisins Soaked in Grappa (page 261). You can construct your own ideal menu with complete confidence. All the recipes here are standouts, the best of the best. Each has been tested and retested in the *Food & Wine* kitchen, and each has made two cuts—first to get into the magazine, and then to be included in this book.

Authentic and stylish home cooking is yours in our *Italian Collection*, along with lots of kitchen tips and excellent, easy-to-understand recommendations from wine expert Mary Ewing-Mulligan of the International Wine Center in New York City. We hope you'll use this convenient volume not only when entertaining friends, but also for everyday Italian feasts.

DANA COWIN
Editor in Chief
FOOD & WINE Magazine

JUDITH HILL
Editor in Chief
FOOD & WINE Books

Fresh Tomato and Basil Pizza, page 190

WINE INTRODUCTION

In Italy, food and wine are inseparable. No matter how simple or humble the meal, wine is there. Sunday dinners, weekday dinners, fancy restaurant meals, and lunches at the kitchen table all feature wine as a necessary ingredient. Even families stopping for a roadside picnic lunch wash their sandwiches down with wine. Of course, these wines are all Italian.

In recent years, Americans have made much ado about the science of marrying wine and food—the contrasting or the matching of flavors, textures, flavor intensities, and weights to create the perfect gustatory experience. But Italians long ago simplified the issue of food and wine pairing. They evidently concluded that the type of wines that go best with food, generally speaking, are wines that are very dry, light- to medium-bodied, not too flavorful in their own right, and not particularly fruity. These are the characteristics that, for the most part, typify the wines of Italy.

The great majority of Italian white wines are light-bodied, dry, crisp wines with low flavor intensity and relatively neutral flavors. (Soave might taste a bit like almonds, of course, while pinot grigio might taste citrusy, but their common characteristics far outweigh their individual traits.) Above all, they have high natural acidity, which enables the wines to cleanse the mouth between bites of food. The net effect of these characteristics is that Italian white wines, generally speaking, provide a refreshing, cleansing foil to the flavors of many, many different foods.

The majority of Italian red wines are medium-bodied, firm, dry wines with moderate flavor intensity and not particularly high levels of tannin, the mouth-drying substance in red wines. Italy's very finest reds—Barolo, Barbaresco, Brunello di Montalcino, and Taurasi— stand out from this norm because they are quite full-bodied, and often very tannic.

Red wines from the south of Italy tend to be a little softer than wines from the north and they usually have more intense flavor, often a flavor of cooked fruit. In the context of all red wines of the world, however, Italy's reds are distinctly un-fruity. At the table, this lack of fruitiness suits the wines perfectly to the types of foods that Italians eat.

In decades past, Italy's isolation from the rest of Europe—surrounded as Italy is by seas and mountains—enabled Italian winemakers to develop their unique style of food-friendly wines so appropriate for the way that Italians themselves appreciate wine. Today, however, for better or for worse, outside influences have begun to encroach on Italian wines.

Rosemary Grissini, page 211

Today's world market demands wines that have intense flavor in their own right, whether the flavor of familiar wine grapes such as chardonnay or cabernet sauvignon that are grown all over the world, or the flavor of toasted oak barrels that the wines age in. Seeking their place on the world stage, some Italian winemakers now make wines to suit these international tastes. As a result, some Italian white wines now have pronounced smoky flavors of oak, and some red wines have intense fruit character along with oaky aromas and flavors.

These newer-style Italian wines can be delicious when you drink them alone, without food, and can also go very well with certain dishes. In addition, they add variety to the repertoire of Italian wine styles. But the intensity of their flavor and the presence of oaky character means that, unlike Italy's typical white and red wines, they do not automatically go well with just about any dish, anytime, anywhere.

It is possible to get more specific about the process of pairing Italian food with wine, especially for Italy's red wines, which are stylistically more varied than her whites. We could mention that lamb often tastes wonderful with Chianti or any other wine based on the sangiovese grape. We could proclaim barbera the perfect wine for any dish that is spicy or has a tomato-based sauce. We could analyze the weight, flavor, and texture of dozens of Italian wines.

But any attempt to codify the food compatibilities of Italian wines would violate the spirit of those wines. Italy's wines exist to be enjoyed with food, and with gusto. Tedious analysis has no place at the Italian table.

MARY EWING-MULLIGAN

ANTIPASTI

Tuscan-Style White Bean Salad, page 30, with
assorted antipasti

ROSEMARY-AND-ORANGE ROASTED PEPPERS

These roasted peppers are delicious on their own, or served with a little of their oil over spaghetti or in room-temperature pasta salads. As the peppers marinate, the flavors will intensify. They will keep in the refrigerator for several weeks.

MAKES ABOUT 1 QUART

12 red bell peppers

2 sprigs fresh rosemary, or 2 bay leaves

2 cloves garlic, crushed

2 strips orange zest

2 to 3 cups olive oil

1. Roast the peppers over an open flame or broil, turning with tongs, until charred all over, about 10 minutes. When the peppers are cool enough to handle, pull off the skin. Quarter the peppers and remove the stems, seeds, and ribs.

2. Place the peppers in a clean, dry 1-quart jar. Add the rosemary, garlic, and orange zest. Pour in the oil, adding enough to cover the peppers and fill the jar. Slide a clean blunt knife blade between the peppers to release any trapped air bubbles. Cover the jar and store in the refrigerator until ready to use.

—DIANA STURGIS

Opposite: Rosemary-and-Orange Roasted Peppers (center, top), and prosciutto-wrapped Sweet-and-Hot Melon (center, below), page 17, surrounded by an assortment of antipasti

MARINATED MUSHROOMS WITH ROASTED RED PEPPERS AND ARUGULA

You can use all white mushrooms if you wish, but fresh shiitakes—or other fleshy wild mushrooms—add a more earthy flavor and varied texture.

SERVES 4 TO 6

⅓ cup extra-virgin olive oil

3 shallots, minced

2 cloves garlic, minced

1 pound white mushrooms, quartered

1 pound shiitake mushrooms, stems removed and caps quartered

¼ cup balsamic vinegar

2 large red bell peppers

1 tablespoon chopped fresh marjoram

1 teaspoon salt

1 teaspoon fresh-ground black pepper

1 bunch arugula (about 2 ounces), stems removed

1. In a large heavy frying pan, heat the oil over moderate heat. Add the shallots and garlic, reduce the heat to low, and cook, stirring occasionally, until softened but not browned, about 5 minutes. Increase the heat to moderately high and add the white and shiitake mushrooms, stirring well to combine. Cover the pan and cook, stirring once, until the mushrooms are slightly softened, about 4 minutes.

2. Uncover, increase the heat to high, add the balsamic vinegar, and cook for 1 minute. Spoon the mushroom mixture into a large bowl and let it cool to room temperature, stirring occasionally.

3. Meanwhile, roast the peppers over an open flame or broil, turning with tongs, until charred all over, about 10 minutes. When cool enough to handle, pull off the skin. Remove the stems, seeds, and ribs. Cut the peppers lengthwise into ½-inch strips.

4. Add the roasted peppers to the mushrooms. Stir in the marjoram, salt, and pepper. Cover and refrigerate the mixture until ready to serve.

5. To serve, arrange the arugula leaves on a large serving plate and spoon the mushroom salad on top. Serve chilled or at room temperature.

—MARCIA KIESEL

SWEET-AND-HOT MELON

Even though this antipasto is made with just a few ingredients, it is full of flavor. For the sweetest cantaloupe, be sure to select one that is ripe: It will have an enticing fragrance and both ends will yield slightly to pressure. Since the flesh next to the seeds has the most intense flavor, take care to remove only the seeds, not the top layer of fruit. For a special treat, substitute a fragrant Cavaillon melon for the cantaloupe. The marinated melon wedges are delicious wrapped in thin slices of prosciutto.

MAKES 16 WEDGES

1 small ripe cantaloupe, halved lengthwise and seeded

½ to ¾ teaspoon dried red-pepper flakes

¼ cup dry Marsala

Pinch salt

1. Cut each melon half lengthwise into 4 wedges. Using a paring knife, remove the rind. Cut each wedge crosswise in half and place in a medium bowl.

2. Add the red-pepper flakes, Marsala, and salt and toss well. Serve, or cover and refrigerate, tossing occasionally, for up to 2 hours.

—ANNE DISRUDE

MARSALA

A favorite fortified Sicilian wine, Marsala is probably most familiar to Americans in the sautéed dish veal Marsala or the simple Italian dessert sauce zabaglione.

Marsala is available in four grades, from Fine, at the lowest end, to Superiore, Superiore Riserva, and Marsala Vergine. The first three may be dry or sweet, but Vergine is always dry. Marsala Vergine is an excellent aperitif; a good Superiore Riserva or Superiore in a sweet style can be good with biscotti or dessert. All Marsala wines are from local Sicilian grape varieties.

RED-WINE-MARINATED SHALLOTS

These shallots are good as soon as they are made, but are even better after several days, when their flavor has fully developed and they've become deep burgundy. They will keep in the refrigerator for several months. Eat them on their own with good crusty bread or as an accompaniment to mortadella or roast pork. When peeling the shallots, barely trim the root end, to keep them intact during cooking.

MAKES ABOUT 30 SHALLOTS

- 1 pound large shallots
- 2 tablespoons sugar
- 1 small sprig fresh rosemary, or ¼ teaspoon dried
- ¼ cup extra-virgin olive oil
- 1 bottle dry red wine (750 ml)
- ⅛ teaspoon coarse-ground black pepper

1. In a medium bowl, toss the shallots with the sugar and rosemary. In a large frying pan, heat the oil. Add the shallots and cook over moderate heat, tossing frequently, until browned, 5 to 7 minutes. Add the wine and pepper and bring to a simmer. Cook until the shallots are tender, 20 to 25 minutes.

2. Using a slotted spoon, transfer the shallots and rosemary sprig, if using, to a 1-quart heatproof jar. Boil the cooking liquid until reduced to 1¼ cups, 10 to 15 minutes. Pour over the shallots. Let cool completely, then cover and refrigerate until ready to serve.

—ANNE DISRUDE

TARRAGON MUSHROOMS

The deep, resonant flavor of this antipasto comes from combining dried porcini with fresh white mushrooms. Serve them tossed with additional chopped fresh tarragon and lemon juice. These mushrooms will keep for several months in the refrigerator.

MAKES ABOUT 20 MUSHROOMS

1 ounce dried porcini mushrooms

1½ cups boiling water

2 tablespoons olive oil

½ small onion, minced

1 pound small fresh white mushrooms

¼ cup tarragon vinegar

1 teaspoon coarse salt

6 sprigs fresh tarragon, or 2 teaspoons dried

1. Put the porcini in a small bowl and pour the boiling water over them. Soak until softened, about 20 minutes. Remove the mushrooms, reserving the soaking liquid, and coarsely chop them. Strain the liquid through a paper-towel-lined sieve into a medium saucepan.

2. In a large frying pan, heat the oil over moderate heat. Add the onion and cook, stirring occasionally, until translucent, about 3 minutes. Add the white mushrooms and cook, stirring occasionally, until warmed through, 1 to 2 minutes. Add the vinegar and cook for 1 minute. Add the porcini and salt and cook for 1 minute longer. Using a slotted spoon, transfer the mushrooms to a 1-quart heatproof jar. Add the tarragon.

3. Bring the reserved porcini liquid to a boil and pour into the jar. Add enough boiling water to fill the jar. Let cool, then cover and refrigerate until ready to serve.

—ANNE DISRUDE

BRAISED CELERY WITH OLIVES

The delicate flavor and texture of cooked celery is often overlooked, but when braised, it makes a tasty and inexpensive antipasto that will keep in the refrigerator for up to two weeks. Or serve it with salmon flaked over the top or with shavings of fresh Parmesan and some extra fresh-ground black pepper.

MAKES ABOUT 4 DOZEN PIECES

- 1 large bunch celery, ribs separated
- 2 tablespoons extra-virgin olive oil
- 3 cloves garlic, crushed
- ⅓ cup Niçoise olives
- 4 bay leaves
  Pinch dried red-pepper flakes
- ½ cup dry white wine
- ½ cup Chicken Stock, page 79, or canned low-sodium chicken broth
- ¼ teaspoon salt
- ¼ teaspoon fresh-ground black pepper

1. Trim the leaves and any bruised ends from the celery ribs. Peel the ribs, then slice lengthwise into ½-inch strips. Cut the strips crosswise into 4- to 5-inch pieces.

2. In a large frying pan or heavy pot, heat the oil over moderate heat. Add the garlic, olives, bay leaves, and red-pepper flakes and cook, stirring frequently, until aromatic, 3 to 5 minutes. Do not let the garlic brown.

3. Increase the heat to high, add the wine, and boil for 1 minute. Add the stock and celery, return to a boil, and reduce the heat to low. Cover and cook, stirring occasionally, until the celery is crisp-tender, about 20 minutes. Remove from the heat.

4. Let the celery cool in the liquid. Season with the salt and black pepper. Transfer the celery and its cooking liquid to a glass dish, cover, and refrigerate until ready to serve.

—ANNE DISRUDE

ITALIAN OLIVE HARVEST

The olive crop is harvested in Italy between the months of November and March. The olives are handpicked by workers on ladders, or the trees are shaken or struck so that the olives fall into large nets laid out on the ground below. Green olives are picked when they are underripe, purple olives when they are just ripe, and black olives when they are overripe.

It is traditional to celebrate the olive harvest with *bruschetta,* grilled slices of bread rubbed with garlic cloves and drizzled with freshly pressed olive oil.

OLIVE-STUFFED PEPPER WEDGES WITH TOMATOES AND ANCHOVIES

This dish is based on a recipe from chef Sandra Gluck, who brought it back from Pierino Govene, chef-owner of Ristorante Gambero Rosso in Cesenatico, on Italy's Adriatic coast. Since it is prepared in advance and served at room temperature, this antipasto couldn't be easier.

MAKES 16 WEDGES

- 5 canned plum tomatoes, drained and chopped
- 10 to 12 Kalamata or other brine-cured black olives, pitted and chopped
- 3 tablespoons chopped flat-leaf parsley
- 2½ tablespoons capers, rinsed and chopped
- 3½ tablespoons extra-virgin olive oil
- 2 to 3 anchovy fillets, chopped
- 2 cloves garlic, minced
- ½ teaspoon fresh-ground black pepper
- 2 large red bell peppers
- 2 large yellow bell peppers

1. Heat the oven to 375°. In a medium bowl, combine the tomatoes, olives, parsley, capers, 1½ tablespoons of the oil, the anchovies, garlic, and black pepper.

2. Cut the peppers in half lengthwise and remove the stems, seeds, and ribs. Make two diagonal crisscross cuts in each half to form 4 triangular wedges.

3. Lightly oil a large shallow baking dish and arrange the pepper pieces in a single layer, hollow-sides up. Spoon 1 heaping teaspoon of the olive stuffing into each piece. Cover the dish with foil.

4. Bake until the peppers begin to soften, about 15 minutes. Uncover and bake until they are tender but not limp, about 10 minutes longer. Let cool to room temperature.

5. Transfer the stuffed pepper wedges to a serving platter and drizzle with the remaining 2 tablespoons oil.

—RICHARD SAX

Apulian Eggplant Rolls

These eggplant rolls are from Apulia, the region that forms the heel of the Italian boot. They make a wonderful antipasto or a delicious luncheon dish. Serve them at room temperature to enjoy their fullest flavor.

SERVES 6 TO 8

- 1 large eggplant (about 2 pounds), cut lengthwise into ¼-inch slices
  Salt
- 2 cups olive oil
- ¼ cup dry bread crumbs
- 3 cloves garlic, minced
- ½ cup chopped fresh parsley
- 1¼ cups grated mozzarella
- ½ cup grated Parmesan cheese
- 1 large egg, beaten
  Fresh-ground black pepper
- 1 cup Marinara Sauce, page 128

1. Layer the eggplant slices in a colander, sprinkling the layers with 1 tablespoon salt. Set aside to drain for at least 1½ hours. Gently squeeze out the excess liquid. Pat dry with paper towels.

2. In a large frying pan, heat the oil over moderately high heat to 375°, or until a small bread cube browns in about 1 minute. Add the eggplant slices in small batches and fry, turning once, until golden and cooked through, about 2 minutes per side. Remove and drain on paper towels.

3. Heat the oven to 375°. In a medium bowl, combine the bread crumbs, garlic, parsley, mozzarella, and 6 tablespoons of the Parmesan. Stir in the egg and season with salt and pepper.

4. Spoon ¼ cup of the sauce into an 8 by 12-inch stainless-steel or glass baking dish. Spread about 1 tablespoon of the mozzarella mixture on one end of each slice of eggplant, roll up, and place seam-side down in the pan.

5. Bake the eggplant until the sauce bubbles and the cheese is melted, about 20 minutes. Serve hot or at room temperature with the remaining sauce and Parmesan.

—Nancy Verde Barr

Make It Ahead

You can assemble this dish several hours ahead and keep covered at room temperature. Then bake it shortly before you are ready to serve.

FIGS AGRODOLCE

Italians love to pickle vegetables and fruits for antipasti, and figs are no exception. They make an excellent sweet-tart accompaniment to prosciutto and other cured meats. Since the pickled figs become increasingly vinegary and their liquid increasingly sweet, it is best to use them within two weeks.

MAKES ABOUT 2 DOZEN FIGS

1 pound dried figs, stemmed

2 cups red-wine vinegar

2 to 3 strips orange zest

1. Put the figs into a stainless-steel saucepan. Add the vinegar and enough water to cover. Add the orange zest, cover, and simmer over low heat until the figs are very soft, about 2 hours.

2. Remove from the heat. Let the figs cool in the liquid. Transfer the figs and their cooking liquid to a glass bowl or jar, cover, and keep at room temperature until ready to serve.

—ANNE DISRUDE

HOMEMADE HERBED RICOTTA CHEESE

The full yet delicate flavor of freshly made ricotta is a real treat, and it is easy and quick to prepare. For this delicious antipasto, the fresh cheese is highlighted with sprinklings of salt and pepper, rosemary, green olives, and a small amount of extra-virgin olive oil. Serve with crackers or thinly sliced Italian bread.

MAKES ABOUT 1 CUP

1   quart milk

½   cup heavy cream

1   tablespoon plus 1 teaspoon lemon juice

Pinch dried rosemary

⅛   teaspoon salt

⅛   teaspoon fresh-ground black pepper

2   brine-cured green olives, pitted and minced

2   teaspoons extra-virgin olive oil

1. In a large stainless-steel saucepan, bring the milk and cream to a boil over high heat. When the liquid is boiling vigorously, stir in the lemon juice; the mixture will separate into curds and whey in 5 to 10 seconds.

2. Immediately remove from the heat and drain in a fine sieve lined with a double thickness of dampened cheesecloth. Discard the liquid. Transfer the ricotta to a small plate and let cool, uncovered, at room temperature.

3. With the back of a spoon, spread the ricotta in an even layer on the plate. Sprinkle with the rosemary, salt, pepper, and olives. Drizzle the oil over the cheese.

—ANNE DISRUDE

RICOTTA CHEESE

Ricotta, which translates as "recooked," is a by-product of the whey left over after cheesemaking, particularly provolone and mozzarella. It is used extensively in Italian cooking, as a topping or filling for pasta dishes and in pastries and cheesecakes. It also is eaten plain, sprinkled with sugar and cinnamon or cocoa, and enjoyed with fresh fruit.

Fresh ricotta should be purchased and used within a few days of being made. Factory-made ricotta, which lacks the creamy texture and pure flavor of fresh, has a longer shelf life.

HERBED MOZZARELLA

This recipe always works well as long as you use good fresh mozzarella and extra-virgin olive oil. Fresh mozzarella is available at Italian markets, many fine cheese shops, and some supermarket deli counters. Either fresh or dried herbs can be used here, or a combination—it all depends on what's on hand. The dried herbs listed below, for example, can be augmented with or replaced by 1 tablespoon each of chopped fresh basil, chives, and parsley. Grate or chop a cube or two of this flavored cheese and sprinkle over room-temperature pan-grilled zucchini or eggplant, or serve it over a bed of shredded Belgian endive and radicchio.

MAKES 16 TO 20 PIECES

- 1 pound fresh whole-milk mozzarella, either tiny bocconcini or 1 large ball
- ½ cup extra-virgin olive oil
- 1 teaspoon dried thyme
- ½ teaspoon dried oregano
- ½ teaspoon fresh-ground black pepper
- ¼ teaspoon dried red-pepper flakes
- ¼ teaspoon dried rosemary
- 1 teaspoon coarse salt

1. If using a large ball of cheese, cut it into 1-inch cubes. Put the mozzarella into a medium bowl. Add the oil, thyme, oregano, pepper, red-pepper flakes, rosemary, and salt; toss to coat evenly.

2. Cover and refrigerate for at least 1 hour, or up to 2 weeks, tossing occasionally. Remove from the refrigerator about 30 minutes before serving.

—ANNE DISRUDE

FRESH MOZZARELLA

In Italy, the coveted water-buffalo's milk mozzarella is rarely used for cooking. Instead, it is purchased at its prime—one day old, tender, and dripping with whey—and tossed with tomatoes, olive oil, and fresh basil leaves. Or it is served unadorned as a dessert.

However, there are also practical reasons for not cooking with any type of fresh mozzarella—cow's milk or water-buffalo's milk. Because the fresh cheese is still so soft and full of whey, it cannot be easily sliced or grated and it contributes too much liquid and not enough flavor when it is cooked with other ingredients. An Italian cook planning to use fresh mozzarella in a cooked dish will "age" the cheese for several days to let it give up some of its moisture, making it firmer and its flavor more concentrated.

Ricotta Salata with Hot Peppers and Lemon

In Italy, cheese is served both before the meal and afterward with fruit. For this simple and rustic antipasto, aged sheep's-milk cheese is sliced and marinated with hot peppers, lemon, and olive oil. Sharp-flavored black olives make a nice accompaniment.

MAKES 16 TO 20 PIECES

12 small green or red Italian hot peppers

 1 pound ricotta salata or feta cheese, sliced 1 inch thick

    Zest of 2 lemons, removed in strips

½ cup extra-virgin olive oil

Make It Ahead

You can layer the cheese, peppers, and lemon zest up to 3 weeks ahead. Cover and refrigerate. When ready to serve, bring to room temperature.

---

1. Roast the peppers over an open flame or broil, turning with tongs, until charred all over, about 7 minutes. When the peppers are cool enough to handle, pull off the skins, trying not to tear the peppers.

2. Put half the cheese slices in the bottom of a 2- to 3-quart shallow glass dish. Top with half the lemon zest and half the roasted peppers. Drizzle ¼ cup of the oil over the peppers. Repeat with the remaining cheese, lemon zest, peppers, and oil. Cover and let stand at room temperature for at least 30 minutes for the flavors to infuse.

3. To serve, break the cheese into 1-inch pieces or cut into thin triangles. Mince the peppers and lemon zest and sprinkle over the top.

—Anne Disrude

FRITTATA WEDGES

This Italian open-faced omelet will take any number of fillings, such as artichokes, zucchini, or leftover pasta. You can also vary the flavoring. For example, substitute 1 tablespoon minced fresh basil and parsley or 1 tablespoon minced roasted red pepper and 1 teaspoon minced parsley for the pepperoni.

MAKES 6 OR 8 WEDGES

- 2 large eggs
- 1 tablespoon minced pepperoni
- 1 teaspoon chopped fresh parsley
- ⅛ teaspoon salt
- Pinch fresh-ground black pepper
- 1½ teaspoons extra-virgin olive oil

1. In a small bowl, beat together the eggs, 2½ teaspoons of the pepperoni, ¾ teaspoon of the parsley, the salt, and pepper.

2. Place a 7-inch frying pan over moderately high heat. Add the oil and swirl to coat the bottom of the pan. Add the egg mixture and swirl to coat the bottom of the pan. Reduce the heat and cook, without stirring, until the top is set but soft, 3 to 4 minutes.

3. Carefully slide the frittata onto a dinner plate, then invert back into the pan. Cook until completely set, about 30 seconds. Slide the frittata back onto the plate.

4. Cut into 6 or 8 wedges and serve hot or at room temperature, garnished with the remaining ½ teaspoon pepperoni and ¼ teaspoon parsley.

—ANNE DISRUDE

MAKE IT AHEAD

You can make the frittata 1 to 2 hours ahead. Let it cool, then cover and leave at room temperature until ready to serve.

MARINATED WHITE BEANS

Tuscans are very fond of beans and enjoy them hot, cold, and at room temperature. This dish of simply marinated cannellini, dressed with additional olive oil, is typical Tuscan fare.

SERVES 6 TO 8

1 pound (about 2½ cups) dried white beans, preferably cannellini, or chickpeas

2 ribs celery

1 onion, halved

Bouquet garni: 1 bunch parsley stems, 1 small sprig fresh rosemary or ½ teaspoon dried, 7 sprigs fresh sage or ½ teaspoon dried, 2 bay leaves, and 1 small dried red chile pepper

½ cup extra-virgin olive oil, plus more for serving

1 teaspoon salt

½ teaspoon fresh-ground black pepper

Lemon wedges, for serving

1. Soak the beans or chickpeas overnight in enough cold water to cover by at least 2 inches. Or, bring the beans to a boil, cover, remove from the heat, and let sit for 1 hour. Drain.

2. Put the beans in a medium pot with enough cold water to cover by at least 2 inches. Add the celery, onion, and bouquet garni. Bring to a boil, reduce the heat, and simmer, partially covered, until the beans are soft but still hold their shape, about 1½ hours for white beans or 2½ hours for chickpeas. Drain well and spread on a large baking sheet to cool. Remove and discard the vegetables and bouquet garni.

3. Toss the beans or chickpeas with the oil, salt, and pepper. Serve with additional oil and lemon wedges.

—ANNE DISRUDE

VARIATION

WHITE BEANS WITH CALAMARI

In a medium saucepan of lightly salted boiling water, blanch 1½ pounds cleaned calamari for 1 minute. Drain and cut the bodies into ¼-inch rings. Put the calamari into a medium bowl. Add 1½ cups Marinated White Beans, 3 tablespoons olive oil, 3 tablespoons chopped fresh parsley, 2 tablespoons lemon juice, ½ teaspoon salt, and ¼ teaspoon fresh-ground black pepper.

TUSCAN-STYLE WHITE BEAN SALAD

While this dish makes a delicious antipasto or an accompaniment to almost any simple meat, it also can be offered as the centerpiece of a compose-your-own salad. Present the beans, surrounded by tomato wedges, with an assortment of tasty components for each guest to choose from: tuna packed in olive oil, good black olives, crisp greens, scallions, sliced cucumbers, and the like.

SERVES 6 TO 8

¾ pound (about 2 cups) dried cannellini or Great Northern beans

1 small yellow onion

2 cloves garlic

4 sprigs fresh sage or thyme, or ¼ teaspoon dried thyme

4 plum tomatoes

2½ teaspoons salt

1 teaspoon fresh-ground black pepper

1 small red onion, chopped

1 small rib celery with leaves, cut into ¼-inch dice

¼ cup thinly sliced scallion greens

2 tablespoons shredded fresh basil

1 tablespoon chopped fresh parsley

⅓ cup extra-virgin olive oil

3 tablespoons lemon juice

1. Soak the beans overnight in enough cold water to cover by at least 2 inches. Or, bring the beans to a boil, cover, remove from the heat, and let sit for 1 hour. Drain.

2. Put the beans in a medium pot with enough cold water to cover by at least 2 inches. Add the yellow onion, garlic, and 2 sprigs of the sage or thyme, if using. Bring to a boil, reduce the heat, and simmer, partially covered, until the beans are tender but not mushy, about 1½ hours. Drain the beans; discard the onion, garlic, and sage.

3. Meanwhile, core and seed 1 tomato and cut it into ½-inch dice. Cut the remaining 3 tomatoes into 6 wedges each. Finely chop the remaining 2 sprigs of sage or thyme, if using.

4. Put the beans into a large bowl and season with the salt and pepper. Add the chopped tomato, the red onion, the celery, scallion greens, basil, parsley, the chopped sage or thyme or dried thyme, the olive oil, and lemon juice. Toss gently with two rubber spatulas to combine the ingredients without crushing the beans. Cover and set aside for at least 1 hour to blend the flavors.

5. Transfer the beans to a serving bowl or platter and surround with the tomato wedges. Serve at room temperature.

—RICHARD SAX

Tuscan-Style White Bean Salad with assorted antipasti

INSALATA DI MARE

Delicately flavored seafood salads are enjoyed throughout Italy, although they differ depending on what the local waters offer. This salad uses clams, shrimp, scallops, and calamari, but certainly more of one seafood can be used in favor of another. The most important thing for the success of the dish is that the seafood be of the very best quality.

SERVES 4

1 pound boiling potatoes (about 3 medium), peeled and cut into 1-inch chunks

½ cup dry white wine

1 shallot, thinly sliced

4 sprigs flat-leaf parsley

6 black peppercorns
  Salt

8 small clams, such as Manila or littleneck, scrubbed

4 large shrimp (about ¼ pound), shelled and deveined

4 sea scallops (about 3 ounces)

¾ pound cleaned calamari, bodies cut into ¼-inch rings, tentacles cut in half

¼ cup extra-virgin olive oil

1 cup chopped bell pepper (red, yellow, or green)

1 teaspoon dried oregano
  Fresh-ground black pepper

6 fresh basil leaves, thinly sliced
  Lemon wedges, for serving

1. Put the potatoes in a medium saucepan of salted water. Bring to a boil, reduce the heat, and simmer until tender, about 8 minutes. Drain.

2. In a large stainless-steel saucepan, combine 4 cups of water, the wine, shallot, parsley, peppercorns, and ½ teaspoon of salt. Bring to a boil over high heat, reduce the heat to moderate, and simmer for 10 minutes.

3. Add the clams to the pan and cook just until they open, 3 to 5 minutes. Using a slotted spoon, remove the clams to a large bowl as they open. Discard any that do not open.

4. Cook the remaining seafood in the simmering broth, one type at a time, removing it to the bowl of clams with the slotted spoon: about 1½ minutes for the shrimp, 2 minutes for the scallops, and 1 minute for the calamari, or just until the seafood is tender and cooked through.

5. Gently toss the seafood together. Stir in the oil, bell peppers, oregano, and potatoes. Season with 1 teaspoon salt and ½ teaspoon black pepper. Mix gently and season with additional salt and pepper to taste.

6. To serve, mound the salad on four plates and sprinkle the basil on top. Serve with lemon wedges.

—TONY MANTUANO, MANGIA,
KENOSHA, WISCONSIN

PANCETTA-WRAPPED SCALLOPS WITH LEMON

Pancetta lends a dash of saltiness to the sweet scallops and protects them from direct heat in this simple broiled antipasto. You can substitute 8 to 10 strips of sliced bacon for the pancetta. If you do, cut each strip into 3-inch lengths.

MAKES 2 DOZEN PIECES

6 large sea scallops (about ½ pound), quartered

3 tablespoons extra-virgin olive oil

4 3-inch strips lemon zest, plus 1 teaspoon grated zest, for garnish

2 fresh rosemary sprigs, plus 2 teaspoons chopped, for garnish

Fresh-ground black pepper

12 thin slices pancetta (about ¼ pound), halved crosswise

1. In a medium bowl, toss the scallops with the oil, lemon zest strips, and rosemary sprigs. Season with pepper. Cover and refrigerate, tossing occasionally, for 2 hours. In a small bowl, soak 24 wooden toothpicks in water for 2 hours.

2. Heat the broiler. Remove the scallops from the marinade and lightly pat them dry. Wrap each piece of scallop in a slice of pancetta, secure with a toothpick, and transfer to a broiler pan. Broil the scallops, turning once, until the pancetta sizzles and the scallops are just done, about 1 minute.

3. In a small bowl, combine the grated lemon zest and chopped rosemary. Dip one end of each scallop in the lemon-herb mixture, transfer to a platter, and serve.

—CAPERS CATERING, CHICAGO

ANTIPASTO DI PESCE

There are three categories of Italian antipasto. An *antipasto misto* (mixed antipasto) can include all of the antipasto possibilities. An *affettato* is just sliced pork products, such as salami—a sort of Italian cold-cut platter. And an *antipasto di pesce* is seafood only. It might include a variety of seafood salads, stuffed mussels, clams or squid, and such simple preparations as fish marinated in olive oil and lemon juice or a sweet-and-sour sauce.

CARPACCIO WITH PARMESAN SHAVINGS

Carpaccio is paper-thin sliced raw beef that is often served drizzled with olive oil and fresh lemon juice. Here, the meat is drizzled with balsamic vinegar and olive oil, topped with fresh mushrooms and Parmesan cheese, and served on crisp toast. Freezing the meat for about an hour will help make it easier to shave off thin slices.

MAKES 24 SMALL CROSTINI

12 slices country-style round Italian bread, halved crosswise, or 24 slices from a long loaf

¾ pound lean top round, cut into 24 paper-thin slices

2 tablespoons balsamic vinegar

2 tablespoons extra-virgin olive oil
   Salt and fresh-ground black pepper

¼ pound porcini or cremini mushrooms, sliced paper-thin

¼ pound Parmesan cheese, thinly sliced

2 tablespoons chopped flat-leaf parsley

1. Heat the oven to 375°. On a large baking sheet, toast the bread in the oven until crisp and golden, about 10 minutes.

2. Top each piece of toast with a slice of beef, folding it over to fit as necessary. Sprinkle lightly with the vinegar and oil. Season lightly with salt and pepper.

3. Top each toast with several mushroom slices, some Parmesan, and a sprinkling of parsley. Arrange on a platter and serve.

—LORENZA DE'MEDICI

BALSAMIC VINEGAR

Balsamic vinegar, made from the cooked and concentrated must of white grapes, has been produced in Modena and Reggio Emilia for hundreds of years. A dark-brown, wine-based vinegar with a heady fragrance and sweet-sour flavor, *aceto balsamico tradizionale* must, by law, be aged for a minimum of ten years and is sometimes aged for up to fifty years or longer. To develop its distinctive flavor, it is transferred through a series of twelve kegs made of different aromatic woods, including juniper, mulberry, chestnut, and red oak, as it ages.

This distinctive vinegar has long been cherished. In fact, it was once considered so valuable that it was included in the dowries of young ladies of nobility and was specifically mentioned in wills.

GRILLED PROSCIUTTO AND FONTINA CHEESE PANINI

These bite-size sandwiches, filled with prosciutto, Fontina cheese, and fresh herbs, are so appetizing they will appeal to everyone.

MAKES 8 PANINI

4 not-too-thin slices prosciutto (about 3 ounces)

8 ¼-inch slices Italian or French bread (about 3 inches in diameter)

¼ pound Italian Fontina or mozzarella cheese, shredded

4 fresh sage or basil leaves

About ¼ cup extra-virgin olive oil

1 large clove garlic, crushed

1 small fresh or dried hot chile pepper

1 lemon, quartered

Sprig of fresh sage or basil, for garnish

1. Fold a slice of prosciutto to fit on each of four slices of the bread. Top with the cheese and sage leaves. Cover with the remaining four slices bread.

2. In a large frying pan, heat ¼ cup oil with the garlic and chile pepper over moderate heat. When the garlic sizzles, carefully add the sandwiches to the pan. Fry until the bottoms are golden, about 4 minutes. With a wide spatula, turn the sandwiches over. Add a little more oil if needed, reduce the heat slightly, and fry until the second side is golden and the cheese is melted but not runny, about 3 minutes.

3. Place the sandwiches on a serving plate and cut them in half. If desired, warm the oil remaining in the pan and drizzle a little of the seasoned oil over the sandwiches. Garnish with the lemon quarters and sage sprig. Serve hot.

—RICHARD SAX

MAKE IT AHEAD

You can put these appetizer sandwiches together a couple of hours before serving if you like. Cover with plastic wrap and keep at room temperature. Then toast in the frying pan when ready to serve.

PARMESAN CROSTINI

Crostini are among the most popular antipasti in Italy. They are simply toasted bread slices topped with a variety of ingredients. For a holiday antipasto, serve these crostini with an array of cheeses. The herbed oil is also a fine addition to salad dressings, or use it for oil-brushed breads such as focaccia.

MAKES 4 DOZEN CROSTINI

1   teaspoon dried rosemary

1   teaspoon dried thyme

½   teaspoon dried red-pepper flakes

2   bay leaves, crushed

½   cup olive oil

1   10-ounce loaf Italian bread

¼   cup grated Parmesan cheese

1. In a small bowl, combine the rosemary, thyme, red-pepper flakes, bay leaves, and oil. Cover and let stand at room temperature for at least 12 hours.

2. Cut the bread into three 4-inch lengths. Wrap individually and freeze for at least 4 hours, or overnight.

3. Defrost the bread for 10 to 15 minutes. Trim off the ends and cut the bread into ¼-inch slices.

4. Heat the oven to its lowest setting. Arrange the bread slices in a single layer on a wire rack set in a large baking sheet. Bake until dry but not browned, about 30 minutes.

5. Increase the oven temperature to 250°. Lightly brush one side of the toast with the herbed oil. Sprinkle the Parmesan over the oiled side of each toast and bake until golden brown and crisp, about 1 hour.

—DIANA STURGIS

WILD MUSHROOM CROSTINI

In Italy, this recipe is prepared with the succulent wild mushrooms called porcini. A good substitute for those expensive delicacies is cremini or fresh shiitake mushrooms, both of which are available in specialty food shops and some supermarkets. The dish is still quite flavorful when made partially or entirely with ordinary white button mushrooms.

MAKES 12 TO 16 CROSTINI

- ¾ pound wild mushrooms, such as porcini, cremini, or shiitake
- 3 tablespoons unsalted butter
- 1½ tablespoons olive oil
- 1 clove garlic, minced
- 2 tablespoons chopped fresh parsley
  Salt and fresh-ground black pepper
- 2 tablespoons dry Marsala
- 1 tablespoon heavy cream
- 12 to 16 slices Italian bread, toasted

1. If using shiitakes, remove the stems. Coarsely chop the mushrooms. In a large frying pan, melt the butter with the oil over high heat. Add the mushrooms, garlic, and parsley. Cook, stirring frequently, until the mushrooms absorb the fat, 1 to 2 minutes. Reduce the heat to low and season with ½ teaspoon salt and several grindings of pepper. Cook, stirring occasionally, until the mushrooms begin to release their juices. Increase the heat to moderate and cook, stirring occasionally, until the juices evaporate, about 6 minutes.

2. Add the Marsala and cook until reduced to 1 tablespoon, scraping the bottom of the pan to dislodge any browned bits.

3. Transfer the mushrooms and any liquid to a food processor and puree to a paste, about 1 minute. With the machine running, gradually add the cream. Taste and add salt and pepper if necessary. (The puree should taste slightly oversalted while still warm.) Transfer the puree to a bowl and let cool completely.

4. Just before serving, generously spread the mushroom puree over the toasted bread.

—TOM MARESCA AND DIANE DARROW

MAKE IT AHEAD

You can make the mushroom puree up to a day in advance. Cover and refrigerate. Let come to room temperature before serving.

TOMATO-BASIL CROSTINI

Serve these crostini in the summer when vine-ripened, flavorful tomatoes and fresh basil are abundant.

MAKES 24 SMALL CROSTINI

1½ pounds plum tomatoes (8 to 9 medium), quartered

Salt

1 clove garlic, minced

1 tablespoon chopped fresh basil

2 tablespoons chopped flat-leaf parsley

¼ cup extra-virgin olive oil

Fresh-ground black pepper

12 slices country-style round Italian bread, halved crosswise, or 24 slices from a long loaf

1. Put the tomatoes in a food processor and pulse until coarsely chopped; do not puree. Transfer the tomatoes to a colander or strainer and toss with 1 teaspoon salt. Let drain for 1 hour, stirring once or twice.

2. Heat the oven to 375°. In a medium bowl, combine the tomatoes, garlic, basil, and parsley. Gradually whisk in the oil until well blended. Season with more salt if necessary and pepper.

3. Put the bread on a large baking sheet and toast in the oven until crisp and golden, about 10 minutes.

4. Put the tomato mixture in a small bowl in the center of a platter and surround with the toasted bread.

—LORENZA DE'MEDICI

CROSTINI WITH TARRAGON EGG SALAD

Tarragon is common in Siena but is practically unknown in the rest of Italy. For this antipasto, the anise-flavored herb is combined with capers, hard-cooked eggs, and olive oil to make a savory mixture that can be spread on toast or served as a dip. The bread for the crostini should have a firm texture and good crust.

MAKES 24 SMALL CROSTINI

¼ cup chopped fresh tarragon or flat-leaf parsley

2 tablespoons capers, chopped

2 hard-cooked eggs, chopped

¼ cup extra-virgin olive oil

   Salt and fresh-ground black pepper

12 slices country-style round Italian bread, halved crosswise, or 24 slices from a long loaf

1. Heat the oven to 375°. In a medium bowl, combine the tarragon, capers, and eggs with a fork. Gradually whisk in the oil until well blended. Season with salt and pepper to taste.

2. Put the bread slices on a large baking sheet and toast in the oven until crisp and golden, about 10 minutes.

3. Spread each slice with the tarragon mixture and arrange on a platter. Alternatively, spoon the spread into a small bowl and surround with the toasts.

—LORENZA DE'MEDICI

MAKE IT AHEAD

You can make the tarragon egg salad spread a day ahead. Keep it covered in the refrigerator. The olive oil will prevent the tarragon from discoloring.

Opposite: Crostini with Tarragon Egg Salad (left) and Carpaccio with Parmesan Shavings (right), page 35

FIRST COURSES

Garlic-Shrimp Risotto, page 74

LIGURIAN VEGETABLE SOUP

Soups play an important role in the Italian menu, often taking the place of pasta as a first course or served as a light main course for supper. This recipe is best if the vegetables aren't cut too small, since the finished soup should have a chunky look. Fresh vine-ripened tomatoes—peeled, seeded, and chopped—can be used in place of the canned tomatoes called for in the recipe.

WINE RECOMMENDATION

Red wines and oaky white wines are both out of consideration here because the bitter greens and the acidic tomatoes in this soup would react unfavorably with the tannin of the wine. Try a light-bodied Italian white wine that is not oaked, such as Soave, Orvieto, or Frascati.

SERVES 8

¼ cup extra-virgin olive oil

1 large onion, coarsely chopped

2 ribs celery, coarsely chopped

2 carrots, coarsely chopped

1 pound Savoy or green cabbage, coarsely shredded or chopped

2 teaspoons salt

½ teaspoon fresh-ground black pepper

2 cups coarsely shredded romaine lettuce or escarole

1 pound boiling potatoes (about 3 medium), peeled and cut into ½-inch dice

1¼ cups canned plum tomatoes, drained and coarsely chopped

4 cups Vegetable Stock, page 77, or canned low-sodium chicken broth

1 cup shelled fresh or frozen peas

⅓ cup chopped flat-leaf parsley

2 cloves garlic, minced

8 to 10 slices Italian bread, toasted

Grated Parmesan cheese, for serving

1. In a large saucepan, heat the oil over moderate heat. Add the onion, celery, and carrots and cook, stirring often, until softened, about 10 minutes. Add the cabbage, salt, and pepper and cook, stirring, until the cabbage is wilted, about 3 minutes. Add the lettuce and cook until wilted, about 1 minute. Stir in the potatoes and tomatoes and cook for another 3 minutes.

2. Increase the heat to moderately high, add the stock, and bring to a boil. Reduce the heat to moderately low, cover, and simmer for 30 minutes. Add the peas and cook, covered, for 5 minutes. Combine the parsley and garlic and stir into the soup; cook for 5 minutes.

3. Put a piece of toasted bread in each soup bowl. Ladle the hot soup on top and serve with a light sprinkling of the Parmesan.

—NANCY VERDE BARR

ZUCCHINI AND ARBORIO RICE SOUP

In Italy, this thick, hearty soup is often served at room temperature. The flavors will blend while it sits and cools. It makes a delicious first course for a menu including fish.

■ WINE RECOMMENDATION
The combination of relatively light flavors and substantial weight in this dish calls for a crisp white wine whose acidity will cut the food's heaviness, and a wine with mild flavors that don't overpower the food. Fortunately, these characteristics apply to almost every Northern or Central Italian white wine that is not barrel-aged.

SERVES 6 TO 8

¼ cup extra-virgin olive oil

1 onion, chopped

1 clove garlic, minced

1½ pounds zucchini (about 3 medium), cut into ½-inch dice

¼ teaspoon grated nutmeg

2 teaspoons salt

¼ teaspoon fresh-ground black pepper

1½ cups canned plum tomatoes, drained and chopped

6 cups Vegetable Stock, page 77, or canned low-sodium chicken broth

1 cup arborio rice

3 tablespoons chopped flat-leaf parsley

3 tablespoons chopped fresh basil

Grated Parmesan cheese, for serving

1. In a large saucepan, heat the oil over moderately low heat. Add the onion and garlic and cook, stirring occasionally, until softened but not browned, about 8 minutes.

2. Add the zucchini and season with the nutmeg, salt, and pepper. Increase the heat to moderate and cook, stirring occasionally, until the zucchini is barely tender, about 10 minutes.

3. Add the tomatoes, stock, rice, parsley, and basil. Increase the heat to moderately high and bring the soup to a boil. Reduce the heat to moderately low and simmer until the rice is tender, about 20 minutes. Serve hot or at room temperature with the Parmesan.

—NANCY VERDE BARR

TUSCAN BREAD SOUP

Rustic bread soups are among the most humble and delicious soups served in Italy. When making this dish, which is more like a porridge than a soup, the bread should be squeezed very dry after it is soaked. The soup can be served at room temperature in warm weather or hot in the winter, to warm the bones.

WINE RECOMMENDATION
The flavors of this soup are strong enough to accommodate a red wine, but tannic reds could be a problem with the tomato. The barbera grape is low in tannin, however; a medium-bodied Barbera d'Asti would work well.

SERVES 6 TO 8

1   loaf (1 pound) crusty Italian bread, preferably Tuscan, several days old, cut into 1-inch cubes (about 8 cups)

¾   cup olive oil, plus extra for serving

3   large cloves garlic, minced

8   large fresh sage leaves, chopped

3   14-ounce cans Italian-style peeled tomatoes, drained

5½ cups Beef Stock, page 78, or canned low-sodium beef broth, boiling

Salt and fresh-ground black pepper

1. Put the bread in a large bowl and sprinkle with about 4 cups of cold water, making sure the bread is evenly moistened. Let soak until all of the water is absorbed, about 10 minutes. Using your hands, squeeze the bread as dry as possible. Separate the bread into pieces.

2. Heat the oil in a large pot. Add the garlic and sage and cook over moderate heat, stirring occasionally, until the garlic begins to color, about 4 minutes. Add the bread and toss constantly with a wooden spoon until the cubes are well coated with oil, about 5 minutes.

3. Put the tomatoes in a food mill fitted with the fine disk and puree them directly into the casserole. Alternatively, puree the tomatoes in a food processor and strain through a sieve into the pot to remove the seeds. Mix until well blended.

4. Stir in the boiling broth, season with salt and pepper, and return to a boil. Remove from the heat and stir. Cover the pot and set aside for 1 hour.

5. Using a wooden spoon, stir the soup to break up most of the remaining lumps of bread. Season with salt and pepper. Reheat over low heat if desired. Spoon the soup into bowls and drizzle about 1 teaspoon of olive oil over each serving.

—GIULIANO BUGIALLI

PORCINI MUSHROOM SOUP WITH PARMESAN TUILES

This creamy mushroom soup is topped with steamed milk in the style of cappuccino. If you can't find fresh porcini, substitute an additional ounce (4½ tablespoons) of porcini powder. Alternatively, use 1 ounce of dried porcini that have been reconstituted and chopped; add them with the cremini.

WINE RECOMMENDATION
This soup needs a wine that complements its earthy flavors and also has enough of an edge to cut through the soup's creaminess. Dolcetto, from Piedmont—a very dry red wine that is often served with antipasti—should come alive with the soup, and vice versa.

SERVES 4

2 tablespoons olive oil

1 onion, coarsely chopped

2 teaspoons minced garlic

¼ pound fresh porcini mushrooms, stems removed and caps coarsely chopped

¼ pound cremini mushrooms, stems removed and caps coarsely chopped

¼ cup dry sherry

2 cups Chicken Stock, page 79, or canned low-sodium chicken broth

1½ tablespoons porcini powder* or finely ground dried porcini mushrooms (⅓ ounce)

6 tablespoons grated Parmesan cheese

2 cups heavy cream

2 tablespoons butter

1 cup milk

4 fresh chives, minced

*Available at specialty food stores

1. In a large frying pan, heat the oil over moderate heat. Add the onions and garlic and cook, stirring occasionally, until the onions are translucent, about 5 minutes. Add the mushrooms, raise the heat to moderately high and cook, stirring occasionally, until lightly browned, about 5 minutes. Add the sherry and bring to a boil. Boil until the liquid has reduced to a glaze. Add the stock and porcini powder and bring to a boil. Boil until reduced by half, about 5 minutes. Remove from the heat and let cool.

2. Transfer the mushroom mixture to a blender or food processor and puree. Strain the soup into a medium saucepan.

3. Heat the oven to 350°. On a nonstick baking sheet, spread one quarter of the cheese evenly into a 3 by 2-inch oval. Repeat with the remaining cheese to make a total of 4 ovals, leaving about 3 inches between them. Bake until the cheese is

melted and golden, 4 to 5 minutes. Working quickly, remove the tuiles with a wide metal spatula and drape them over a rolling pin. Let cool.

4. Add the cream to the soup and bring to a simmer over moderate heat; do not boil. Whisk in the butter.

5. Steam the milk in a cappuccino machine according to the manufacturer's instructions. Alternatively, whisk the milk in a medium saucepan over moderately low heat until foamy and steaming hot, about 5 minutes.

6. Pour the soup into four cappuccino cups or small soup bowls. Spoon the foamy milk on top and garnish with the chives. Serve the Parmesan tuiles alongside.

—RICK TRAMONTO AND GALE GAND,
TRIO, EVANSTON, ILLINOIS

MAKE IT AHEAD

You can make the soup through step 2 up to 2 days ahead. Cover and refrigerate.

ITALIAN GREENS WITH TOMATOES

In Italy, many meals end with a salad that has a slightly bitter and refreshing taste. Italian greens such as escarole, chicory, and arugula have those qualities. You could use radicchio, Belgian endive, or frisée here as well.

WINE RECOMMENDATION
Conventional wisdom dictates that you have this salad with no wine at all, because of its high acidity and bitterness— but who wants a whole course without wine? Fortunately, barbera, the amazingly flexible red wine from Piedmont, will work well even here.

SERVES 4

½ small red onion, thinly sliced

1 tablespoon red-wine vinegar

1 teaspoon balsamic vinegar

¼ teaspoon salt

¼ teaspoon fresh-ground black pepper

2 quarts bite-sized pieces mixed Italian greens, such as escarole, arugula, and chicory

3 small tomatoes, cut into thin wedges

3 tablespoons olive oil

1. In a small bowl, toss the onion with the red-wine vinegar, balsamic vinegar, salt, and pepper.

2. In a large salad bowl, toss the greens and tomatoes with the olive oil. Add the onion mixture, toss again, and serve.

—TRACEY SEAMAN

GRILLED RADICCHIO STUFFED WITH MOZZARELLA

Small heads of radicchio stuffed with mozzarella and topped with chopped anchovies, red-pepper flakes, and olive oil make a stunning side dish or first course for a meal featuring pasta. The faintly sweet mozzarella provides a nice contrast to the slightly bitter radicchio.

WINE RECOMMENDATION
This scrumptious dish calls for a white wine that has a suggestion of sweetness, to balance the earthy, bitter character of the radicchio. Barrel-aged white wines often take a little sweetness from the oak, and one could work here. Try an oaked chardonnay, whose earthy flavors would echo the earthiness of the dish.

SERVES 4

4 small heads radicchio (about 1 pound)

4 bocconcini (miniature mozzarella balls)

4 small anchovy fillets, coarsely chopped
    Salt and fresh-ground black pepper
    Dried red-pepper flakes

2 teaspoons chopped flat-leaf parsley
    Extra-virgin olive oil, for drizzling
    Lemon wedges, for serving

1. In a medium saucepan of boiling, salted water, blanch the heads of radicchio until wilted, 2 to 3 minutes. Using a slotted spoon, remove to a colander. Gently press out as much water as possible. Drain well on paper towels.

2. Light the grill or heat the broiler. Gently pull open the leaves of each head of radicchio and place a ball of mozzarella in the center. Top the cheese with the anchovies and season with salt, black pepper, and a pinch of red-pepper flakes. Sprinkle with parsley and a few drops of oil. Carefully enclose the cheese in the leaves. Secure each bundle with two toothpicks.

3. Lightly brush the radicchio with olive oil. Grill or broil, turning once, until the radicchio is golden brown, about 6 minutes.

4. Transfer the radicchio to a serving platter. Remove the toothpicks and garnish with lemon wedges.

—VIANA LA PLACE

MIXED GREENS WITH POLENTA AND GORGONZOLA CROUTONS

Polenta flavored with Gorgonzola cheese is a delectable Venetian dish. Here the two ingredients combine as a savory, crisp garnish for a flavorful Italian green salad of fresh seasonal greens in a light vinaigrette.

WINE RECOMMENDATION
Because the greens in this dish are particularly bitter, you need a soft white wine that will counterbalance the bitterness. Greco di Tufo, from the Southern Italian region of Campania, will do the trick.

SERVES 6

- 3 cups water
- 1¼ teaspoons salt
- 1 cup coarse or medium cornmeal
- 1 head radicchio
- 1 small head chicory (curly endive)
- 1 small head romaine lettuce
- 1 large Belgian endive
- 1 tablespoon red-wine vinegar
- 3 tablespoons plus ⅓ cup olive oil, preferably extra-virgin
- 1 tablespoon walnut oil
- ½ teaspoon Dijon mustard
- ⅛ teaspoon fresh-ground black pepper
- 4 ounces Gorgonzola cheese, at room temperature

1. In a medium saucepan, bring the water and ¾ teaspoon of the salt to a boil. Add the cornmeal in a slow, steady stream, whisking constantly. Reduce the heat to moderate. Simmer, stirring frequently with a wooden spoon, until the polenta is very thick and pulls away from the sides of the pan, about 20 minutes.

2. Oil a large baking sheet. Using a lightly oiled wooden or plastic spatula, spread the polenta onto the prepared baking sheet in an even rectangle about 12 by 6 by ¼ inch. Let cool to room temperature, then cover and refrigerate until well chilled.

3. Meanwhile, prepare the salad greens. Cut the core from the radicchio and separate the head into individual leaves. Separate the chicory and romaine into individual leaves, remove the tough ribs and tear the leaves into bite-size pieces. Separate the Belgian endive into separate spears. Combine the greens, rinse thoroughly, and dry.

4. In a small bowl, whisk together the vinegar, 3 tablespoons of the olive oil, the walnut oil, mustard, the remaining ½ teaspoon salt, and the pepper.

5. Heat the broiler. Cut the polenta into six 6 by 2-inch rectangles. In a large frying

pan, heat the remaining ⅓ cup olive oil over moderately high heat. Add the polenta and cook, turning once, until crisp and golden, about 4 minutes. Remove with a slotted spatula and drain on paper towels. Spread the Gorgonzola on the fried polenta.

6. In a large bowl, toss the greens with the vinaigrette until coated. Divide the salad among six plates.

7. Broil the polenta croutons until the cheese melts, about 1 minute. Slice each rectangle crosswise into 6 smaller rectangles or cut into triangles and arrange on top of the salads.

—John Robert Massie

Polenta

Polenta is a staple in the Veneto region and some of the other far northern parts of Italy. It is traditionally made in a deep copper pan, called a *paiolo*, that is suspended over an open fire, and is stirred with a special long-handled spoon made of chestnut or acacia wood. When it is cooked, the piping-hot polenta is first poured onto a white cloth and then placed on a wooden board. Polenta is traditionally cut with a wooden spatula or a thick cotton thread.

Gorgonzola

Gorgonzola, named after a village near Milan, has been produced in the Po Valley since the 9th century. Along with English Stilton and French Roquefort, it is considered one of the top three blue cheeses in the world, although the characteristic veining of this celebrated cheese is actually more green than blue. Sweet, young Gorgonzola (aged only four to six months) is rich and creamy; the aged version, which can be up to one year old, is even more robust.

ARUGULA AND BASIL SALAD WITH PARMESAN SHAVINGS

Peppery arugula, shredded basil and slivers of Parmesan make a tempting light first course before a substantial main dish of meat or pasta, or a refreshing salad at the end of a meal.

WINE RECOMMENDATION
Just about any inexpensive, unoaked white Italian wine, such as Frascati, Soave or a modest pinot grigio, will be subtle enough not to clash with this salad, and light enough that you can follow with a fuller white wine or a red for your next course. Alternatively, try a dry amontillado sherry from Spain—a much fuller and more flavorful partner that will bring nutty richness to the dish.

SERVES 4

- 2 tablespoons balsamic vinegar
- ½ teaspoon salt
- ¼ teaspoon fresh-ground black pepper
- 3½ tablespoons extra-virgin olive oil
- 2 small bunches arugula (about ½ pound), stems removed
- 12 large fresh basil leaves, coarsely shredded
- 1 2-ounce chunk Parmesan cheese, for shaving

1. In a large bowl, whisk together the the vinegar, salt, and pepper. Whisk in the oil until blended.

2. Add the arugula and basil and toss to coat. Arrange the salad on plates. Using a vegetable peeler, cut the chunk of Parmesan into thin shavings. Top the salads with the Parmesan shavings.

—STEPHANIE LYNESS

ARUGULA

Also known as rugula, Italian cress, and rocket, arugula is a delicate salad green used frequently in Mediterranean dishes. When young, its long, tender leaves have a pleasant peppery flavor. Mature arugula has a stronger, more assertive flavor that can be bitter. You can use arugula leaves exclusively to make a full-flavored salad or as an accent with other milder-tasting greens.

PANZANELLA

Thrifty Italian cooks have developed a subcuisine based on leftovers, from roast meat and poultry to pasta and bread. Bread in particular has inspired a number of famous solutions, including *panzanella*, or bread salad. *Panzanella* is traditionally made of Tuscan bread, a salt-free, chewy Italian loaf, which dries rock-hard.

WINE RECOMMENDATION The flavors here are so lively, fresh, and assertive that you need a wine with a strong personality of its own. Either a riesling or a traminer wine from the Alto Adige or Friuli region would be a strong candidate.

SERVES 8

- 1 loaf (1 pound) crusty Italian bread, preferably Tuscan
- 4 medium tomatoes (about 1½ pounds), cut roughly into ½-inch cubes
- 1 large cucumber, peeled and thinly sliced
- 5 scallions, chopped (about 1 cup)
- ¼ cup chopped fresh basil
- 6 tablespoons olive oil, preferably extra-virgin
- 3 tablespoons red-wine vinegar
- 1 teaspoon salt
- 1 teaspoon fresh-ground black pepper

1. Three days before making the salad, cut the bread roughly into 1-inch cubes and leave out, uncovered, turning several times, so that it becomes stale and hard.

2. To make the salad, spread the stale bread cubes in a large, shallow baking dish; the bread should be no more than two cubes deep. Drizzle 4 cups of cold water over the bread, moistening all the cubes. Let soak for 10 minutes—no longer.

3. Squeeze as much water as possible from the bread. Put the bread on one half of a large kitchen towel and pat out to about ¼ inch. Fold the towel over to cover the bread, slide onto a baking sheet, and chill for about 2 hours.

4. Meanwhile, put the tomatoes, cucumber, scallions, and basil in a large salad bowl. Cover and chill.

5. Transfer the cold bread to a dry towel. Form into a long, narrow cylinder; roll it up in the towel and twist to squeeze out as much water as possible.

6. Remove the vegetables from the refrigerator. Tear off small pieces of the bread and crumble it into the salad.

7. In a small bowl, whisk together the oil, vinegar, salt, and pepper. Pour the dressing over the salad. Rake a fork through the salad to mix and serve chilled.

—HELEN MILLMAN

ARTICHOKES WITH GARLIC AND FRESH MINT

Serve these Roman-style artichokes with sturdy bread to soak up the juices. They make a lovely introduction to a meal of fish or poultry. Use an enameled cast-iron pot with a tight-fitting lid for cooking the artichokes. They should fit as snugly as possible in the pot.

WINE RECOMMENDATION
Common wisdom suggests that you don't even try to match artichokes with wine. An unconventional choice such as a brut Italian sparkling wine, however, should work with this dish.

SERVES 4 TO 6

- 4 medium artichokes
- 12 sprigs fresh mint
- ½ teaspoon salt
- ½ teaspoon fresh-ground black pepper
- ½ cup extra-virgin olive oil
- 8 cloves garlic, peeled

1. Cut off the artichoke stems and any spiny leaf tips. Rinse the artichokes. Pull open the centers and stuff 3 mint sprigs into each one. Put the artichokes in a heavy pot just large enough to accommodate them. Sprinkle with the salt and pepper and drizzle with the oil. Add the garlic cloves and ¼ cup of water.

2. Bring to a boil, reduce the heat to moderately low, and cook, covered, adding water as necessary to maintain a simmer, until the bases of the artichokes are tender when pierced with a small knife and a leaf pulls out easily, about 40 minutes. Let the artichokes cool in the pot.

3. To serve, remove the mint sprigs and set aside. Using a pair of scissors and beginning at the tips, quarter each artichoke lengthwise. Or quarter the artichokes with a large sharp knife. Carefully remove the chokes with a spoon and discard them. Put the artichokes on a plate. Chop the mint sprigs and garlic cloves together and mix with the pan juices. Pour the mixture over the quartered artichokes, and serve.

—ANNE DISRUDE

MAKE IT AHEAD

You can cook the artichokes up to 10 days ahead. Leave them whole and let cool in the pot, then cover and refrigerate.

VEGETABLE CARPACCIO

For this refreshing starter, nearly transparent slices of vegetables are enhanced with a tangy caper dressing. Slicing the vegetables paper-thin allows the juices locked in the fibers to come to the surface and encourages the absorption of the dressing. Use a mandoline-type slicer to ensure neat, thin shavings.

WINE RECOMMENDATION
Although the idea of serving wine with raw vegetables is a bit unorthodox, the right wine could pleasantly surprise your guests. Because Italian white wines are so light, this is one occasion to look elsewhere for the richness and character necessary to match the complex personality of the dish. Try a dry riesling from France's Alsace region, from one of the producers who makes it in a firm, crisp style, such as Trimbach or Leon Beyer.

SERVES 4

- 4 large radishes
- 1 large carrot
- 1 rib celery from the heart
- 1 leek, white and light-green parts only
- 1 small fennel bulb, halved and cored
- 3 tablespoons lemon juice, plus ½ lemon
- 1 teaspoon Dijon mustard
- 3 tablespoons extra-virgin olive oil, plus more for drizzling
- 1 heaping tablespoon small capers
  Salt
- 1 medium artichoke
- 1 2-ounce chunk Parmesan cheese, for shaving
  Fresh-ground black pepper

1. Using a mandoline-type slicer, very thinly slice the radishes, carrot, celery, leek, and fennel bulb.

2. In a large bowl, combine the lemon juice and mustard and beat lightly with a fork. Beat in the oil. Stir in the capers and season with salt.

3. Trim the artichoke, rubbing the cut portions with the lemon half as you go. Cut the stem off the artichoke. Pull off all the dark-green outer leaves around the base. Cut the artichoke crosswise about 1½ inches from the base to remove the remaining leaves. Scoop out the hairy choke and trim any dark green remaining around the top and bottom of the heart.

4. Slice the artichoke heart very thin and toss with the dressing. Add the sliced vegetables and toss gently.

5. Arrange the carpaccio on plates or a platter. Using a vegetable peeler, cut the chunk of Parmesan into thin shavings. Top the carpaccio with the Parmesan shavings. Season with the pepper, drizzle with oil, and serve.

—VIANA LA PLACE

STEWED SPRING VEGETABLES

Make this dish in the springtime when fresh peas, artichoke hearts, and fava beans couldn't be better. As the vegetables simmer, their sweet juices combine with wine and chicken broth for a distinctive flavor.

WINE RECOMMENDATION

The sweetness of this dish calls for a high-acid, unoaked white wine that is very dry, such as a sauvignon blanc or a dry riesling. An inexpensive brand won't have the character to hold its own; go for a better bottle, from an area known for its superior whites, like Friuli or Alto Adige.

SERVES 4

1¼ pounds fava beans, shelled

1 ounce thinly sliced pancetta or prosciutto, finely chopped

1 tablespoon olive oil

1 tablespoon butter

1 pound fresh sweet peas, shelled (about 1½ cups)

½ cup water

1 artichoke

Juice of ½ lemon

1 small onion, coarsely chopped

½ head romaine lettuce, finely shredded crosswise

1½ cups Chicken Stock, page 79, or canned low-sodium chicken broth

⅓ cup dry white wine

Salt and fresh-ground black pepper

1. Peel the fava beans by splitting the skins with your thumbnail and popping out the tender beans.

2. In a medium saucepan, cook the pancetta in the oil and butter over low heat for 1 minute. Add the favas, peas, and water, cover, and cook until the vegetables are tender, about 15 minutes. Drain, reserving the cooking water.

3. Prepare the artichoke by breaking off the tough outer leaves until you reach the yellowish cone of softer leaves. Cut off the cone of leaves flush with the heart. Cut off the artichoke stem and trim off all the dark green parts from the heart. Scoop out the fuzzy choke. Quarter the heart and cut each quarter into sixths. In a small bowl, toss the artichoke wedges with the lemon juice.

4. In a medium enameled cast-iron or stainless-steel pot, combine the artichoke wedges, onion, and lettuce. Add the stock and wine. Cover and cook over low heat until the artichoke wedges are tender, about 25 minutes. Add the peas, fava beans, and their cooking water and simmer until thickened, about 10 minutes longer. Season with salt and pepper and serve.

—LA CAMPANA, ROME

NEAPOLITAN STUFFED PEPPERS

For this recipe, red bell peppers are preferable—their sweet flavor contrasts with the saltiness of the filling. Let the stuffed peppers sit for one day before serving for the flavors to develop fully. Serve them hot or cold as a first course, or place the peppers on top of pasta and dress with the pan juices.

WINE RECOMMENDATION
The wonderful vegetal and earthy flavors of these peppers will really sing when they are echoed by the flavors of the wine. A sauvignon blanc from Tuscany or elsewhere in Italy would be lovely.

SERVES 4

- 8 small red bell peppers
- 6 tablespoons extra-virgin olive oil
- ½ large onion, chopped
- 3 cloves garlic, chopped
- 3 tablespoons chopped fresh parsley
- 4 plum tomatoes, peeled, seeded, and chopped
- 1 teaspoon tomato paste
- 3 tablespoons chopped brine-cured black olives
- 3 tablespoons dry bread crumbs
- 1½ tablespoons chopped capers
- 16 anchovy fillets

1. Using a small sharp knife, cut around the pepper stems, making as small an opening as possible. Pull out the cores. Use a teaspoon to remove the seeds and ribs.

2. Heat the oven to 350°. In a medium frying pan, heat ¼ cup of the oil over moderate heat. Add the onion, garlic, and parsley and cook, stirring, until the onion is translucent, 2 to 3 minutes.

3. Add the tomatoes, tomato paste, and olives and cook until the liquid evaporates, about 5 minutes. Add the bread crumbs and capers. Cook, stirring, for 1 minute.

4. Spoon the filling into the peppers. Put 2 anchovy fillets in each. Spread the remaining 2 tablespoons oil in a baking dish just large enough to hold the peppers. Arrange the peppers in the dish and bake, uncovered, until they collapse, about 1½ hours. Serve the peppers hot, at room temperature, or chilled.

—ANNE DISRUDE

MAKE IT AHEAD

You can prepare these peppers up to a week ahead. Refrigerate in an airtight container.

SCALLOPS VENETIAN-STYLE

In Venice, this dish is usually prepared using large sea scallops with their crimson roe attached—and the flavor is matchless. It is still very good, however, prepared without the roe, as long as the sea scallops are very fresh. This recipe is typical of Italian seafood cookery—it is simple, using minimal preparation to showcase high- quality ingredients.

WINE RECOMMENDATION
The delicacy of this dish begs for a similarly delicate wine, such as the white wine called Gavi from the Piedmont region. Like the dish, Gavi is very elegant.

SERVES 4

- 5 tablespoons butter
- 3 tablespoons minced shallots
- 1 pound sea scallops, with roe if available, cut horizontally into thirds
- ¼ cup dry white wine
- ¼ cup water
- 4 slices firm-textured white bread, toasted and quartered on the diagonal into triangles

1. In a large frying pan, melt 3 tablespoons of the butter over low heat. Add the shallots and cook, stirring occasionally, until softened but not yet browned, about 3 minutes.

2. Increase the heat to moderately high, add the scallops, and cook, stirring constantly (and gently if the roe is attached), for 1 minute. Add the wine and water. Reduce the heat to low, cover, and cook until the scallops are just barely opaque throughout, about 2 minutes.

3. Using a slotted spoon, transfer the scallops to a warm plate and cover with foil to keep warm. Boil the liquid in the pan over high heat until it is reduced to a thick syrup, about 2 minutes. Remove from the heat and stir in the remaining 2 tablespoons butter to make a creamy sauce.

4. Divide the scallops among four plates. Spoon the sauce over them and garnish with the toast points. Serve immediately.

—TOM MARESCA AND DIANE DARROW

MUSSELS MARINARA

As you might expect in a country surrounded on three sides by water, seafood figures prominently in the Italian diet. Steamed mussels served with a broth of tomatoes, garlic, and herbs is a traditional and simple dish in Southern Italy. Serve the dish with good crusty bread or hard pepper biscuits for dipping into the sauce.

WINE RECOMMENDATION
The acidity of the tomatoes precludes any wine that is tannic (it would become astringent with the food)—thus eliminating most reds and oaky whites from consideration. A relatively full-bodied unoaked white wine, such as Lacryma Christi from Southern Italy, would be a good bet.

SERVES 4

⅓ cup extra-virgin olive oil

4 large cloves garlic

3 dozen mussels, scrubbed and debearded

1 35-ounce can crushed tomatoes

1 tablespoon chopped fresh parsley

1 tablespoon chopped fresh oregano, or 1 teaspoon dried

Salt and fresh-ground black pepper

1. In a large pot, heat the oil over moderate heat. Add the garlic and cook, stirring, until lightly browned, 3 to 5 minutes.

2. Add the mussels, tomatoes, parsley, and oregano. Bring to a boil. Reduce the heat to moderate, cover, and simmer, stirring occasionally, until the mussels open, 5 to 7 minutes.

3. Using a slotted spoon, transfer the mussels to soup bowls. Discard any that do not open. Season the sauce with salt and pepper. Ladle the sauce over the mussels and serve hot.

—AMERIGO'S, THE BRONX, NEW YORK

MUSSELS

The most common mussel in North America is the North Atlantic blue mussel. Its shell is dark blue and it is 2 to 3 inches long. In Europe, where the appetite for mussels is much greater than in America, the Mediterranean mussel is prevalent. It also has a blue-black shell, but it is broader than the blue mussel and is marketed at a 3-inch length. Mediterranean mussels, which have a more delicate flavor and creamier texture than our Atlantic blue mussels, are now cultivated in Puget Sound and are available at some fish markets or by mail order.

MUSSELS WITH HERBED CRUMB TOPPING

This makes an excellent first course for guests, because the mussels can be assembled a day ahead, then just broiled for several minutes before serving. Small clams such as cherrystones can also be prepared this way.

WINE RECOMMENDATION Try an earthy-tasting white wine with accents of mineral flavor to complement the earthy, herby flavors of this dish. A good, unoaked Vernaccia di San Gimignano will work well.

SERVES 6 TO 8

2 dozen mussels, scrubbed and debearded

1 tablespoon butter

2 tablespoons extra-virgin olive oil

1 tablespoon minced garlic

1 teaspoon dried oregano

1 cup dry bread crumbs

3 tablespoons chopped flat-leaf parsley

2 tablespoons grated Parmesan cheese

¼ teaspoon salt

¼ teaspoon fresh-ground black pepper

1. In a large pot, bring 1 cup water to a boil over high heat. Add the mussels, cover, and cook, shaking the pot occasionally, just until the mussels begin to open, 5 to 7 minutes. Remove the open mussels and continue to cook, removing the mussels as their shells open. Discard any that do not open.

2. In a small saucepan, melt the butter with the oil over moderate heat. Add the garlic and oregano and stir occasionally until fragrant, about 2 minutes. Remove from the heat, stir in the bread crumbs and parsley, and let cool. Stir in the Parmesan cheese, salt, and pepper.

3. Remove and discard the top shells from the mussels. Arrange the mussels in their bottom shells on a baking sheet. Spoon 1 heaping teaspoon of the bread-crumb mixture onto each one.

4. Heat the broiler. Broil the mussels until golden brown and heated through, 3 to 5 minutes. Arrange on a platter and serve immediately.

—TRACEY SEAMAN

MAKE IT AHEAD

The mussels can be prepared through step 3 up to a day ahead. Cover the baking sheet with foil and refrigerate. Remove from the refrigerator about 30 minutes before broiling.

SPICY CALAMARI SALAD

You can serve these pleasantly chewy calamari as the first course of an extravagant seafood menu, or make the salad a light meal with plenty of crusty bread to dip in the dressing.

WINE RECOMMENDATION
A chilled glass of dry, crisp white wine will cool off the heat of the garlic and red pepper but won't overwhelm the subtle flavor of the calamari. Try a good-quality Verdicchio, such as a single-vineyard version.

SERVES 6

⅔ cup extra-virgin olive oil

⅓ cup lemon juice, or more to taste

4 cloves garlic, minced

¾ teaspoon dried red pepper flakes, or more to taste

4 inner ribs celery with leaves, minced (1¼ cups)

20 pimiento-stuffed green olives, quartered crosswise

Sea salt

2 pounds cleaned calamari, bodies cut into ¼-inch rings, tentacles cut in half

1. In a medium bowl, combine the oil, lemon juice, garlic, and red pepper flakes. Stir in the celery and olives.

2. In a large saucepan, bring 3 quarts of water to a boil. Add 2 tablespoons salt. Add the calamari and cook just until opaque, not more than 1 minute. (Begin testing the calamari after about 30 seconds.) Drain. Transfer the hot calamari to the olive dressing and toss to coat. Cover and refrigerate, tossing occasionally, for at least 3 hours, or overnight.

3. Season with salt and serve chilled or at room temperature.

—PATRICIA WELLS

RICE WITH PEAS

This is a classic Venetian dish that is always served in early spring. This ambrosial combination absolutely requires sweet peas—the younger, the better. If your peas aren't fresh off the vine, you might want to add a pinch of sugar to the pot, or use the best-quality tiny frozen peas. The finished dish should be slightly soupy, not as thick as a true risotto.

WINE RECOMMENDATION
The run-of-the-mill Italian white wines would be overwhelmed by the sweetness of the peas in this dish. Try a better wine made from grapes with good ripeness and concentration: a pinot grigio or chardonnay from the Alto Adige area, especially one from a serious producer such as Alois Lageder.

SERVES 4

- 6 cups Chicken Stock, page 79, or 3 cups canned chicken broth plus 3 cups water
- 4 tablespoons butter
- 2 tablespoons olive oil
- ¼ cup chopped onion
- ½ cup chopped fresh parsley
- 2 ounces pancetta, cut into ¼-inch dice
- 2 pounds fresh peas, shelled, rinsed and drained, or one 10-ounce package tiny frozen peas
- 1 cup arborio rice
- 3 tablespoons grated Parmesan cheese
- 1 teaspoon salt
- ¼ teaspoon fresh-ground black pepper

1. In a medium saucepan, bring the stock to a simmer and keep at a simmer over moderately low heat.

2. In a large saucepan, melt 2 tablespoons of the butter with the oil over moderate heat. Add the onion, parsley, and pancetta. Cook until the fat is rendered from the pancetta and the onion is softened but not browned, about 3 minutes.

3. If you are using fresh peas, add them to the pan and cook for 1 minute, stirring to coat them with the fat in the pan. Gradually add 1½ cups of the hot stock. Reduce the heat to low and simmer, stirring frequently, until the peas are just tender, 15 to 20 minutes.

4. If using frozen peas, add them at this point. Add the remaining 4½ cups stock and bring to a boil. Stir in the rice. Reduce the heat to moderate to maintain a steady simmer and cook, uncovered, stirring occasionally, until the rice is tender but still firm, about 20 minutes.

5. Stir in the remaining 2 tablespoons butter, the Parmesan, salt, and pepper. Simmer for 2 minutes longer, then serve hot.

—TOM MARESCA AND DIANE DARROW

MAKING A PERFECT RISOTTO

There's no mystery to making a perfect risotto, but there are no shortcuts either. This sublime Northern Italian rice dish can be adapted for almost any course of a meal with the addition of various seasonings and ingredients compatible with rice.

Risotto often takes the place of pasta in its area of origin, the regions of Lombardy and Piedmont, where—especially in Milan—it is popular after the theater as a late-night supper dish. It is marvelously versatile, serving as an elegant, rich first course, a sophisticated accompaniment to any number of meat or fish entrées, or even as a dessert. Or, with the addition of some cheese, sausage, or shellfish, or leftovers such as poached fish or sautéed vegetables, it makes a satisfying main course.

The basic technique remains the same for virtually every risotto recipe. The rice (which must be one of the starchy, short-grain varieties, such as arborio) is first stirred in hot fat over heat for a couple of minutes until well coated and slightly translucent. It is then cooked, while being stirred constantly, as a hot liquid—stock, water, wine, or some combination thereof—is gradually added. This is the tricky part, because the total amount of liquid that needs to be added will vary.

The liquid is added about ½ cup at a time—¼ cup at a time near the end—until the rice is al dente and is loosely bound with a thick, creamy sauce. Each addition of liquid is made only when the last has almost evaporated. Too much liquid, and the sauce will be too loose or the rice will become mushy. Too little, and the rice will remain crunchy and may not develop the creamy sauce that is the hallmark of a true risotto.

Other variables include the intensity of heat—the liquid should be maintained at a bare simmer—and the rate of evaporation, which is influenced by the surface area and the material of the pan. Consequently, timing may vary, but a properly cooked risotto will usually take at least 30 minutes.

Don't hesitate to keep testing the rice near the end of the cooking time, to gauge how much more liquid needs to be absorbed. Then, when the risotto is almost done, cheese and other garnishes are added and cooked just long enough to let them warm through. At that moment, act fast. Risotto waits for no one. Pour it into a warm dish and serve immediately, because as it cools, the risotto will tighten and lose its wonderful semifluid consistency.

Risotto alla Milanese

Risotto is perhaps the most beloved dish in the Italian rice repertoire. This classic saffron-tinged risotto is traditionally served with Ossobuco, page 133, but also makes a delicious first course.

WINE RECOMMENDATION
To match the richness of this dish, try a full-bodied, earthy white wine such as a Tuscan chardonnay.

SERVES 4 TO 6

About 5 cups Chicken Stock, page 79, or 2½ cups canned low-sodium chicken broth plus 2½ cups water

Pinch saffron threads

3 tablespoons olive oil

⅓ cup minced onion

2 tablespoons finely diced prosciutto or beef marrow

1½ cups arborio rice

¼ cup dry Marsala or dry white wine

¼ cup grated Parmesan cheese

2 tablespoons butter

Salt

½ teaspoon fresh-ground black pepper

1. In a medium saucepan, bring the stock to a simmer. Crumble in the saffron and keep at a simmer over moderately low heat.

2. In a large saucepan or flameproof casserole, heat the oil over moderate heat. Add the onion and prosciutto and cook, stirring, until the onion is translucent, about 2 minutes.

3. Add the rice and stir until well coated with oil and slightly translucent, 1 to 2 minutes. Add the Marsala and cook, stirring constantly, until it is absorbed, 1 to 2 minutes.

4. Add ½ cup of the simmering stock and cook, stirring constantly, until the stock has been completely absorbed. The stock should bubble gently; adjust the heat as needed. Continue cooking the rice, adding the stock ½ cup at a time and allowing the rice to absorb the stock completely before adding the next ½ cup. Cook until the rice is tender but firm to the bite and the mixture is creamy not soupy, 20 to 25 minutes. (You may not need to use all the stock, or may need more.)

5. Remove the pan from the heat and stir in the Parmesan and butter and season with salt and pepper. Serve hot.

BAKED RISOTTO WITH PROSCIUTTO

Instead of the ring molds, cake pans can be substituted, but in that case, leave the risotto in the oven for a few more minutes. Test by inserting the tip of a knife into the risotto: when the tip is thoroughly hot, it is ready to be served.

WINE RECOMMENDATION
Prosciutto is a tough match for wine, but a crisp white wine with rich texture, such as Tocai Friulano, should work well.

SERVES 12

¼ pound butter, at room temperature

12 thin slices prosciutto

11 cups Chicken Stock, page 79, or canned low-sodium chicken broth

2 tablespoons minced onion

6 cups arborio rice

1 cup grated Parmesan cheese

Salt and fresh-ground black pepper

1. Butter two 6-cup ring molds or two 9-inch cake pans with 1 tablespoon of the butter. Line the pans with the prosciutto, patching with small pieces as necessary.

2. In a medium saucepan, bring the stock to a simmer and keep at a simmer over moderately low heat.

3. In a large pot, melt 3 tablespoons of the butter over moderate heat. Add the onion and cook, stirring frequently, until translucent, about 2 minutes. Add the rice and stir until well coated with butter and slightly translucent, 1 to 2 minutes.

4. Add 3 cups of the simmering stock and cook over high heat, stirring constantly, until most of the stock has been absorbed. Continue cooking the rice, adding the stock 1 cup at a time about every minute and stirring constantly. The rice should always be just covered with a thin layer of stock. After 12 minutes, the rice should be quite dry and tender but still firm.

5. Remove from the heat. Stir in the Parmesan and the remaining 4 tablespoons butter. Season with salt and pepper. Pour the risotto onto a large flat dish to cool completely. Spoon the cooled rice into the prepared molds.

6. Heat the oven to 400°. Bake the risotto on the lowest rack in the oven, uncovered, for 20 minutes. Cover and bake until heated through, about 10 minutes longer. Remove from the oven and let stand for 10 minutes. Carefully unmold onto platters.

—LORENZA DE'MEDICI

Opposite: from left, Baked Risotto with Prosciutto and Veal Rolls with Peas, page 142; Asparagus with Parmesan, page 224; Chicken with Fennel Sauce, page 162, on Spinach with Pine Nuts, page 250

GARLIC-SHRIMP RISOTTO

Wonderfully rich and creamy, this dish can be served as a meal all by itself.

WINE RECOMMENDATION
Shrimp is actually a challenge for most wines. Verdicchio excels with all sorts of seafood and should work well here, thanks to its slightly viscous texture.

SERVES 4 TO 6

5 tablespoons butter

2 cloves garlic, chopped

1 pound medium shrimp, shelled, deveined, and sliced lengthwise

2 tablespoons chopped fresh parsley

5 cups Fish Stock, page 77, or 2½ cups bottled clam juice plus 2½ cups water

1 large leek, white and light-green parts only, split lengthwise, cut crosswise into thin slices, and washed well

1½ cups arborio rice

½ cup dry white wine

½ cup finely julienned carrots

Salt and fresh-ground black pepper

1. In a medium frying pan, melt 2 tablespoons of the butter. Add the garlic and cook over low heat, stirring occasionally, until softened, about 2 minutes.

2. Increase the heat to moderate, add the shrimp and cook, stirring frequently, until just opaque, 1 to 2 minutes. Stir in the parsley.

3. In a medium saucepan, bring the stock to a simmer over moderately low heat.

4. In a large saucepan or flameproof casserole, melt the remaining 3 tablespoons butter over moderate heat. Add the leek and cook, stirring frequently, until softened, 3 to 4 minutes.

5. Add the rice and stir until well coated with butter and slightly translucent, 1 to 2 minutes. Add the wine and cook until it evaporates.

6. Add ½ cup of the simmering stock and cook, stirring constantly, until the stock has been completely absorbed. The stock should bubble gently; adjust the heat as needed. Continue cooking the rice, adding the stock ½ cup at a time and allowing the rice to absorb the stock completely before adding the next ½ cup. Cook until the rice is tender but still slightly crunchy in the center, about 18 minutes.

7. Season with salt and pepper and stir in the shrimp mixture, carrots, and any accumulated juices. Continue to cook, stirring and adding more stock as necessary, ¼ cup at a time, until the rice is tender but still firm and the shrimp are heated through, 3 to 6 minutes longer. Serve hot.

RISOTTO WITH PORCINI MUSHROOMS

The rich, intense woodsy flavor of this risotto dish comes from dried porcini mushrooms—an Italian staple. It makes a good first course or accompaniment to a meal of any roasted meat or poultry.

WINE RECOMMENDATION

Red wine is a logical choice for this earthy, flavorful risotto. Opt for a medium-bodied wine, preferably with herbal flavor accents; Nebbiolo d'Alba or a cabernet from Trentino-Alto Adige are two good choices.

SERVES 4 TO 6

1¾ ounces dried porcini mushrooms

2 cups hot water

6 cups Beef Stock, page 78, or 3½ cups canned low-sodium beef broth plus 2½ cups water

¼ pound butter

1 medium onion, chopped

4 fresh sage leaves, coarsely chopped

2 cups arborio rice

¾ cup dry red wine

3 tablespoons minced fresh parsley

¾ cup grated Parmesan cheese

1. Put the porcini mushrooms in a small bowl and pour the water over them. Soak until softened, about 20 minutes. Remove the mushrooms and strain the liquid through a sieve lined with a paper towel.

2. In a medium saucepan, bring the stock to simmer and keep at a simmer over moderately low heat.

3. Meanwhile, in a large saucepan, melt 6 tablespoons of the butter over moderate heat. Add the onion and sage and cook, stirring occasionally, until the onion is translucent, about 5 minutes. Add the rice and stir until lightly toasted, about 5 minutes.

4. Add the wine and cook, stirring constantly, until the wine is absorbed, about 3 minutes. Stir in the mushrooms and their liquid. Cook, stirring constantly, until the liquid is absorbed, 3 to 5 minutes.

5. Add 1 cup of the simmering stock and cook, stirring constantly, until it is absorbed. The stock should bubble gently; adjust the heat as needed. Continue cooking the rice, adding the stock 1 cup at a time and allowing the rice to absorb the stock completely before adding the next cup. Cook until the rice is tender but firm to the bite and the mixture is creamy but not soupy, about 20 minutes.

6. Remove the pan from the heat and stir in the parsley, Parmesan, and the remaining 2 tablespoons butter. Serve hot.

—CONSTANCE AND ROSARIO DEL NERO

VEGETABLE STOCK

A nice, light base for vegetable dishes, this stock is also a vegetarian alternative to meat, chicken, or fish stock.

MAKES 2 QUARTS

6 onions, chopped

8 carrots, chopped

3 ribs celery, chopped

1 small bunch parsley

4 sprigs thyme, or ½ teaspoon dried

2 bay leaves

1½ teaspoons peppercorns

2½ quarts water

1. Put all of the ingredients in a large pot. Bring to a boil. Reduce the heat and simmer the stock, partially covered, for 45 minutes.

2. Strain. Press the vegetables firmly to get all the liquid. If not using immediately, refrigerate for up to a week.

FISH STOCK

Ask for bones at your fish store. They're often free, and you can get a wealth of flavor from them in minutes.

MAKES ABOUT 1½ QUARTS

3 pounds fish bones, heads, and trimmings

1 onion, chopped

1 carrot, chopped

1½ quarts water

1 cup dry white wine

6 parsley stems

1 sprig thyme, or ⅛ teaspoon dried

1 bay leaf

5 peppercorns

1. Remove any gills from the fish. Rinse the bones, heads, and trimmings well and cut them into pieces.

2. Put all the ingredients in a large pot. Bring to a boil and skim the foam that rises to the surface. Reduce the heat and simmer, uncovered, for 30 minutes.

3. Strain. Press the bones and vegetables firmly with to get all the liquid. If not using the stock immediately, refrigerate for up to 3 days or freeze.

BEEF STOCK

While this stock takes a bit more than 5 hours to make, the actual work time is minimal—less than 20 minutes.

MAKES ABOUT 1½ QUARTS

- 2 pounds beef bones, cut into pieces
- 1 onion, cut into quarters
- 2 carrots, cut into quarters
- 2 ribs celery, cut into quarters
- 2½ quarts water
- 1 14-ounce can (about 1¾ cups) tomatoes, drained
- 8 parsley stems
- 4 sprigs thyme, or ½ teaspoon dried
- 1 bay leaf
- 4 peppercorns

1. Heat the oven to 450°. Put the bones in a large roasting pan. Brown in the oven for 40 minutes, stirring once or twice. Add the onion, carrots, and celery and continue cooking until the bones and vegetables are well browned, about 20 minutes longer.

2. Put the bones and vegetables in a large pot. Pour off all the fat in the roasting pan and add 1 cup of the water. Bring to a boil, scraping the bottom of the pan to dislodge any brown bits. Add to the pot with the remaining 9 cups water, the tomatoes, parsley stems, thyme, bay leaf and peppercorns. Bring to a boil and skim the foam that rises to the surface. Reduce the heat and simmer the stock, partially covered, for 4 hours.

3. Strain. Press the bones and vegetables firmly with a rubber spatula to get all the liquid. Skim the fat from the surface if using the stock immediately. If not, refrigerate for up to a week or freeze and scrape off the fat before using.

VARIATION

VEAL STOCK

Milder in flavor than beef stock, veal stock is made in exactly the same way, with veal bones in place of beef.

CHICKEN STOCK

Make plenty of Chicken Stock while you're at it. It's a great all-purpose stock that you can use in fish and meat dishes as well as in chicken recipes.

MAKES ABOUT 3 QUARTS

- 8 pounds chicken carcasses, backs, wings, and/or necks, plus gizzards (optional)
- 4 onions, cut into quarters
- 4 carrots, cut into quarters
- 4 ribs celery, cut into quarters
- 15 parsley stems
- 10 peppercorns
- 4 quarts of water

MAKE IT AHEAD

You can keep Chicken Stock, as well as Beef and Veal Stock, page 78, and Vegetable Stock, page 77, in the refrigerator for up to a week or freeze it almost indefinitely. Boil it down to half or even less, freeze in small containers, and reconstitute as needed.

1. Put all the ingredients in a large pot. Bring to a boil and skim the foam that rises to the surface. Reduce the heat and simmer, partially covered, for 2 hours.

2. Strain. Press the bones and vegetables with a rubber spatula to get all the liquid. Skim the fat from the surface if using the stock immediately. If not, refrigerate for up to a week or freeze and scrape off the fat before using.

Pasta

Penne with Lamb Ragu, page 102

SPAGHETTINI WITH UNCOOKED TOMATO AND BLACK OLIVE SAUCE

Only ripe, vine-ripened tomatoes and fresh basil will do for this uncooked sauce that is found throughout Italy. Plum tomatoes are the best to use here because they are the meatiest. Use the sauce to dress up any pasta, or serve it with grilled fish, such as swordfish or red snapper.

WINE RECOMMENDATION
The fresh, lively flavors of this dish call for a fuller-bodied, flavorful white wine such as Arneis. Alternatively, a light-bodied barbera, such as an unoaked Barbera d'Asti, would be good.

SERVES 6

1½ pounds very ripe plum tomatoes (about 9 medium), peeled, seeded, and cut into 1½-inch strips

½ cup Gaeta or other oil-cured black olives, halved and pitted

1 large clove garlic, minced

2 tablespoons chopped fresh basil

½ teaspoon salt

¼ teaspoon fresh-ground black pepper

½ cup olive oil

1 pound spaghettini

1. In a large serving bowl, combine the tomatoes, olives, garlic, basil, salt, pepper, and oil. Let stand at room temperature, stirring occasionally, for 1 to 3 hours.

2. In a large pot of boiling, salted water, cook the spaghettini until just done, 8 to 10 minutes. Drain the pasta and toss with the sauce.

—TOM MARESCA AND DIANE DARROW

PASTA COOKING TIPS

• Start with fresh or good-quality dried imported pasta and use ample water—6 quarts for up to 1 pound of pasta. Cover the pot so the water boils quickly.

• Salt the water just before adding the pasta; use about 3½ tablespoons of coarse salt for 6 quarts of water. Water that tastes slightly salty will enhance the flavor of the pasta.

• To prevent pasta from sticking together, stir it frequently during cooking. Never add oil to the water.

• If you are adding pasta to a sauce, undercook it by a minute or two, as it will simmer in the sauce.

• Serve the pasta the moment it's done. To keep it steaming, heat your serving bowls.

—JOHANNE KILLEEN AND GEORGE GERMON

PENNE WITH SWEET PEPPER SAUCE

This recipe is an interpretation of the classic Italian dish of pasta and roasted red bell peppers. Here, the sauce is enhanced with garlic, capers, and olives, for an unforgettable palate-pleaser. A combination of red and yellow peppers makes the most attractive presentation of this dish.

WINE RECOMMENDATION
To match the complex earthy, pungent, and savory flavors of this dish, you need a richly flavored red wine. A Sicilian red, such as Corvo or Regaleali, will have what it takes.

SERVES 6

2 pounds red or yellow bell peppers (about 6 medium), or a combination

¾ cup olive oil

⅓ cup capers, rinsed and coarsely chopped

24 Gaeta or other oil-cured black olives, pitted and quartered

3 cloves garlic, minced

½ cup chopped flat-leaf parsley

⅔ cup dry bread crumbs

1 teaspoon fresh-ground black pepper

1 teaspoon dried oregano

1 pound penne, mezzani, or other tubular pasta

1. Roast the peppers over an open flame or broil, turning with tongs, until charred all over, about 10 minutes. When the peppers are cool enough to handle, pull off the skins. Remove the stems, seeds, and ribs. Cut the peppers into ¼-inch strips.

2. In a large frying pan, heat the oil over moderate heat. Add the roasted peppers, the capers, olives, garlic, parsley, bread crumbs, and black pepper. Mix well, cover, reduce the heat to low, and cook, stirring occasionally, for about 10 minutes. Add the oregano.

3. Meanwhile, in a large pot of boiling, salted water, cook the pasta until just done, 8 to 10 minutes. Drain the pasta and toss with the sauce.

—TOM MARESCA AND DIANE DARROW

PASTA AND ARUGULA WITH TOMATO-OLIVE SAUCE

Pasta with arugula (sometimes called rocket or rugula) is a dish enjoyed in Apulia, the heel of boot-shaped Italy. Here, the pasta is tossed with arugula, a peppery, slightly bitter green, and then the tomato sauce is added. Quick cooking keeps the flavors of the sauce lively.

WINE RECOMMENDATION
The hot red pepper, the peppery arugula, and the pungent black olives give this dish so much flavor that only an assertively flavorful red wine could match its intensity. Try a "super-Valpolicella," a Valpolicella made in the ripasso method, which gives the wine an extra richness of flavor.

SERVES 4 TO 6

- ¼ cup extra-virgin olive oil
- 3 cloves garlic, minced
- ½ teaspoon dried red-pepper flakes
- 1 35-ounce can tomatoes, drained and chopped
- ½ cup Kalamata or other brine-cured black olives, pitted and quartered
- ¼ teaspoon salt
- ¼ teaspoon fresh-ground black pepper
- 1 pound rigatoni
- 2 bunches arugula (about 4 ounces in all), stems removed and coarsely chopped
- Grated Parmesan cheese, for serving

1. In a large stainless-steel frying pan, combine the oil, garlic, and red-pepper flakes. Cook over low heat, stirring occasionally, until the garlic is softened and fragrant, about 3 minutes. Add the tomatoes, olives, salt, and black pepper. Increase the heat to moderately high and simmer until the sauce thickens, about 10 minutes.

2. Meanwhile, in a large pot of boiling, salted water, cook the rigatoni until just done, about 14 minutes. Drain.

3. Put the arugula in a large bowl. Add the pasta and toss well. Add the sauce and toss to coat. Serve with Parmesan on the side

—EVAN KLEIMAN AND VIANA LA PLACE

TAGLIATELLE WITH ASPARAGUS

Italians may love their pasta tender but firm (al dente), but they don't usually like their vegetables cooked that way. This dish is an exception—the asparagus is quickly blanched so it retains some of its crunchiness. Tender, pencil-thin asparagus will work best here.

WINE RECOMMENDATION
The three main flavor ingredients of this dish—asparagus, tomato, and prosciutto—are each tricky with wine on their own, let alone together! A high-acid white wine with a good, rich texture, such as Tocai Friulano, is flexible enough, yet assertive enough to work.

SERVES 6

- 1 pound thin asparagus
- ¼ pound butter
- ¼ pound thinly sliced prosciutto, cut into thin strips
- ⅔ cup drained canned tomatoes, chopped
- ½ teaspoon salt
- 1 teaspoon fresh-ground black pepper
- 1 pound tagliatelle or fettuccine, fresh or dry
- ½ cup grated Parmesan cheese

1. Snap the tough ends off the asparagus and discard them. Cut the spears into 1-inch lengths. In a large pot of boiling, salted water, cook the asparagus until just tender, about 3 minutes. Drain, rinse with cold water, and drain well.

2. In a large frying pan, melt 6 tablespoons of the butter over low heat. Add the prosciutto and cook, stirring occasionally, for 2 minutes. Add the tomatoes, salt, and pepper and simmer until the sauce is slightly thickened, about 5 minutes. Remove from the heat.

3. In a large pot of boiling, salted water, cook the pasta until just done, about 2 minutes for fresh, 8 minutes for dry. Drain and return to the pot.

4. Add the asparagus to the tomato sauce and reheat. Pour the sauce over the pasta, add the remaining 2 tablespoons butter and the Parmesan, and toss well. Transfer to a platter and serve.

—NANCY VERDE BARR

MAKE IT AHEAD

You can blanch the asparagus early in the day, but be sure not to overcook it, so it will keep its bright-green color.

TAGLIATELLE WITH CABBAGE AND SAGE

This hearty and intensely flavored pasta dish of red and napa cabbage, Swiss chard, and fresh sage is reminiscent of Italian peasant cooking. The recipe calls for fresh pasta, but you can use dried. If you do, cook the pasta until almost tender to the bite before adding the greens to the water.

WINE RECOMMENDATION
The rather monochromatic, earthy flavors of this dish will gain a new dimension when a flavorful white wine is paired with them. If you like oaky Italian chardonnays from Tuscany, indulge yourself here.

SERVES 4 TO 6

- ¾ pound fresh tagliatelle or fettuccine
- ¼ medium head red cabbage, thinly sliced crosswise (about 2 cups)
- ¼ medium head napa cabbage, thinly sliced crosswise (about 2 cups)
- ¼ medium bunch Swiss chard, sliced crosswise ¼ inch thick (about 2 cups)
- ¼ pound butter
- 4 cloves garlic, thinly sliced
- 8 fresh sage leaves, thinly sliced lengthwise, or ¼ teaspoon rubbed sage, plus 4 sprigs fresh sage, for garnish (optional)

  Salt and fresh-ground black pepper
- ⅓ cup grated Parmesan cheese

1. Put the pasta into a large pot of boiling, salted water and return to a boil. Stir in the cabbages and the Swiss chard. Cook until the pasta is just done, about 2 minutes. Drain thoroughly and transfer to a large serving bowl.

2. Meanwhile, in a medium frying pan, melt the butter over moderate heat. Add the garlic and sliced sage and cook, stirring occasionally, until the garlic is golden, about 4 minutes.

3. Pour the hot butter mixture over the pasta and vegetables, season with salt and pepper, and toss to mix well. Sprinkle the Parmesan on top. Garnish with the sage sprigs.

—CONSTANCE AND ROSARIO DEL NERO

TAGLIATELLE

Not surprisingly, the lexicon of Italian pasta names is enormous and complex. Even the subtlest change in size or shape or texture seems to require a new pasta term. Tagliatelle—the classic egg noodle from Bologna—on the other hand, has a straightforward, almost generic name. Roughly translated, *tagliatelle* means "cut noodles" (from the verb *tagliare*, "to cut").

BUCKWHEAT PASTA WITH POTATOES, SWISS CHARD, AND ONIONS

Pizzoccheri—brown buckwheat noodles tossed with red potatoes, Swiss chard or cabbage, crisp red onions, and a sauce of Fontina, Parmesan, and garlicky butter—is a traditional dish from the Lombardy region of Italy. Although it would never be served that way in Italy, it makes a wonderful meatless main course. Precede the *pizzoccheri* with pâté, prosciutto, or another cold meat appetizer, and follow with a green vegetable and then with fresh fruit.

WINE RECOMMENDATION
Red or white, the wine that you drink with this delicious, rustic dish must be crisp and refreshing enough to cut through the weight and richness of the food. Try a red wine from Lombardy, where this dish hails from, such as Sassella, Inferno, Grumello, or Valgella—all relatively light-bodied versions of nebbiolo; alternatively, the medium-bodied Gattinara could work.

SERVES 6

- 1 pound small red potatoes, cut into ½-inch chunks
- 1 large bunch Swiss chard, leaves and stems separated
- 6 ounces butter
- 4 cloves garlic, minced
- 2 tablespoons minced fresh sage or oregano, or 1 teaspoon dried oregano
- 1 red onion, diced

  Fresh Buckwheat Pasta, page 92

  Salt and fresh-ground black pepper
- 6 ounces Italian Fontina cheese, grated (about 1½ cups)
- ½ cup grated Parmesan

1. Put the potatoes in a medium saucepan of salted water. Bring to a boil, reduce the heat, and simmer until just tender, about 6 minutes. Drain the potatoes, rinse with cold water, and drain well.

2. Cut the stalks of the Swiss chard crosswise into ½-inch pieces; rinse. Slice the leaves crosswise into thin strips. Put the leaves in a colander and rinse with cold water. Set aside in the colander in the sink.

3. In a medium saucepan of boiling, salted water, cook the chard stalks until just tender, about 4 minutes. Pour the stalks and boiling water over the chard leaves in the colander. Rinse throughly with cold water and let cool. Drain well and squeeze out as much water as possible.

4. Heat the oven to 375°. Butter a large shallow baking dish. In a large frying pan, melt the butter over low heat. Add the garlic and cook, stirring occasionally, until fragrant, about 2 minutes. Add the sage and onion and cook, stirring occasionally, until

the onion is softened, about 5 minutes. Add the potatoes and chard and toss to coat with butter. Cook, covered, until heated through, about 5 minutes.

5. Meanwhile, in a large pot of boiling, salted water, cook the pasta until just done, 10 to 20 seconds if freshly made and 1 to 1½ minutes if the noodles have dried. Drain and transfer to a large bowl. Add the chard mixture and toss gently. Season with salt and pepper. Add the Fontina and Parmesan and toss again.

6. Transfer the pasta to the prepared baking dish. Cover with foil and bake in the upper third of the oven for 10 minutes. Remove the foil and bake until the cheeses are melted and the pasta is heated through, 5 to 7 minutes longer.

—MICHAEL MCLAUGHLIN

CHOOSING CANNED TOMATOES

• Whole peeled tomatoes should not be firm or tinged with green, and there should be lots of tomatoes and a relatively small amount of liquid. Those packed in puree or in juice can be used interchangeably if the recipe calls for drained tomatoes.

• Crushed or chopped tomatoes are an acceptable substitute if you don't want to do your own chopping, but beware of those that have been reduced so much that they are more like a thick puree. In addition, watch out for brands with oregano or basil, which can muddle the flavor.

• Tomato paste should be used judiciously as a thickener or for a touch of color or flavor. It is too concentrated to use in large quantities.

• Tomato sauce—try to avoid using this. It is really nothing more than strained tomatoes and is too thin to make an authentic Italian sauce.

FRESH BUCKWHEAT PASTA

These thick, short noodles, made with eggs and a combination of plain and buckwheat flours, are a specialty of the Valtellina, a valley north of Milan, along the Swiss border.

MAKES 1 ¼ TO 1 ½ POUNDS

- 3 large eggs, at room temperature
- ¼ teaspoon salt
- 1 cup buckwheat flour
- 1 cup all-purpose flour

1. In a small bowl, whisk together the eggs and salt. In a food processor, combine the buckwheat and all-purpose flours. Process briefly to blend. With the machine running, slowly pour in the eggs and process until a firm dough forms, about 10 seconds. Turn the dough out onto a floured work surface (it will be moist and crumbly) and knead until smooth. Wrap the dough in plastic and let rest for 45 minutes before rolling out.

2. Cut the dough into 4 pieces and flatten each piece slightly. Set the rollers of a pasta machine on the widest notch and roll one piece of dough through the machine. Fold the dough over itself lengthwise and roll it through the machine again. Move the setting of the machine to the next notch, fold the dough again, and run it through the machine twice. Continue to flatten the pasta, moving the rollers one notch closer each time, until you've rolled it through the next to the last setting. The pasta should be slightly thicker than regular fettuccine. Let the pasta rest for 25 minutes. Repeat with the remaining dough.

3. Using a fettuccine cutter, cut the pasta into long strips. Trim to 5- to 6-inch lengths. Toss the fettuccine with all-purpose flour to prevent it from sticking and spread it out on a baking sheet. The pasta can be used immediately or stored at room temperature for several days. When the pasta is completely dry, wrap it in plastic.

—MICHAEL MCLAUGHLIN

PASTA WITH FRESH TUNA

This is a fast version of a classic Sicilian dish in which a chunk of fresh tuna is stuffed with mint and garlic and braised in a tomato sauce. The tuna is diced and quickly sautéed, then added to the sauce to finish cooking.

WINE RECOMMENDATION
Red wine is far from automatic with tomato sauces, but the combination of ingredients here seems ideal for one. Make it a light-bodied, low-tannin type, such as Bardolino or an inexpensive sangiovese from Tuscany.

SERVES 4 TO 6

6   tablespoons extra-virgin olive oil

1   large onion, cut into ½-inch dice

1   35-ounce can tomatoes, drained and coarsely chopped

¾   teaspoon salt

½   teaspoon fresh-ground black pepper

1   pound fresh tuna, cut into ½-inch dice

½   cup chopped fresh mint

3   cloves garlic, thinly sliced

1   pound spaghetti or linguine

1. In a large stainless-steel frying pan, heat ¼ cup of the oil over moderate heat. Add the onion, reduce the heat to low, and cook, stirring occasionally, until very soft, 10 to 12 minutes.

2. Add the tomatoes, ½ teaspoon of the salt, and ¼ teaspoon of the pepper. Increase the heat to moderate and cook, partially covered, until the sauce thickens, about 5 minutes. Remove from the heat.

3. Season the tuna with the remaining ¼ teaspoon each salt and pepper. In a medium frying pan, heat the remaining 2 tablespoons oil over moderate heat. Add the tuna and cook, tossing occasionally, until cooked on the surface but still raw in the center, about 4 minutes.

4. Add the tuna, mint, and garlic to the tomato sauce and cook over moderate heat, stirring, until the tuna is just barely opaque throughout, 2 to 3 minutes.

5. Meanwhile, in a large pot of boiling, salted water, cook the spaghetti until just done, about 9 minutes. Drain well and transfer to a large shallow serving bowl.

6. Pour the hot sauce over the pasta and quickly toss to mix.

—EVAN KLEIMAN AND VIANA LA PLACE

LINGUINE WITH SARDINIAN CLAM SAUCE

This highly flavorful clam sauce is from Alghero, Sardinia.

WINE RECOMMENDATION
The exotic nature of this dish calls for a relatively soft white wine. Try a Vermentino di Sardegna or other Sardinian white if you can find one, or a Sicilian white.

SERVES 4 TO 6

2 pounds cherrystone or littleneck clams, scrubbed

½ cup extra-virgin olive oil

4 cloves garlic, minced

½ teaspoon dried red-pepper flakes

1 28-ounce can tomatoes, drained and chopped

¼ cup pitted green olives, quartered

2 tablespoons chopped fresh oregano, or 1 teaspoon dried

2 tablespoons chopped flat-leaf parsley

1 pound linguine

1 cup dry white wine or reserved pasta cooking water

1. Discard any clams that have broken shells or that do not shut when tapped. Soak in lightly salted cold water for 30 minutes. Drain, rinse, and soak in fresh cold water for another 30 minutes. Lift the clams out of the water and rinse with cold water.

2. In a large stainless-steel frying pan or pot, heat the oil over moderate heat. Add the garlic and red-pepper flakes and cook, stirring occasionally, until the garlic is fragrant, about 1 minute.

3. Add the chopped tomatoes, olives, oregano, and 1 tablespoon of the parsley. Cover and cook just until the tomatoes begin to break down, 3 to 5 minutes.

4. In a large pot of boiling, salted water, cook the linguine until just done, about 9 minutes. Drain.

5. Add the clams and wine to the tomato sauce. Cover, increase the heat to high, and cook, shaking the pan occasionally, just until the clams begin to open, about 3 minutes. With a slotted spoon, remove the open clams to a bowl and cover to keep warm. Continue to cook, removing the clams as they open. Discard any that do not open.

6. Add the pasta to the tomato sauce and toss over high heat to allow the pasta to absorb some of the sauce.

7. Transfer the pasta to a large serving bowl. Spoon the clams over the pasta. Pour any sauce in the pan over the clams. Sprinkle with the remaining 1 tablespoon parsley.

—EVAN KLEIMAN AND VIANA LA PLACE

SPAGHETTINI WITH SCALLOPS, PINE NUTS, AND BASIL

Scallops have a sweet, briny flavor that is well suited to the fresh basil in this dish. Here, they are quickly sautéed, releasing their juices, to combine with garlic, olive oil, and toasted pine nuts to make a delicious sauce.

WINE RECOMMENDATION
Rather than trying to match the flavor intensity of this dish, select a fresh, crisp, light-bodied white wine that will let the flavors of the ingredients sing out. A Frascati or Soave would be fine—but do buy the youngest one you can find, to assure its freshness.

SERVES 4 TO 6

¼ cup olive oil, preferably extra-virgin

2 cloves garlic, minced

⅓ cup pine nuts (pignoli)

Salt and fresh-ground black pepper

1 pound spaghettini

1 pound bay scallops

¼ pound butter, melted

¾ cup (packed) fresh basil leaves, coarsely chopped

1. In a large saucepan, heat the oil over moderately low heat. Add the garlic and cook, stirring occasionally, until softened but not browned, about 3 minutes. Add the pine nuts, increase the heat to moderate, and cook, stirring frequently, until the nuts are lightly browned, about 2 minutes. Remove from the heat and season with ½ teaspoon salt and ¼ teaspoon pepper.

2. In a large pot of boiling, salted water, cook the spaghettini until just done, about 9 minutes. Drain.

3. Meanwhile, add the scallops to the sauce. Cook over high heat, stirring frequently, until the scallops are just opaque throughout, 2 to 3 minutes. Remove from the heat and season with a pinch each of salt and pepper.

4. Add the pasta to the sauce and toss to mix. Add the butter and basil and toss again.

—NANCY VERDE BARR

PASTA SALAD WITH BROCCOLI AND TUNA

This authentic Italian salad can be prepared up to three hours before serving. If doing so, do not add the tuna until just before serving. Serve with a salad of mixed greens and Olive Bread, page 209.

■ WINE RECOMMENDATION
Only a white wine could accommodate the tuna fish in this salad. Try a white that has a slightly rich texture, such as a Verdicchio or a Tocai Friulano.

SERVES 8

- 1 head broccoli, cut into tiny florets, stems peeled and cut into bite-size pieces (4 to 4½ cups)
- 1 pound rigatoni
- 2 cups sliced scallions (about 2 bunches)
- 1½ pounds tomatoes (about 3 large), cut into wedges
- 2 7-ounce cans tuna packed in olive oil, drained and coarsely flaked
- 3 cloves garlic, minced
- 3 tablespoons minced flat-leaf parsley
- 2 tablespoons chopped fresh basil
- ½ cup extra-virgin olive oil
- 1 teaspoon salt
- ½ teaspoon fresh-ground black pepper

1. In a large saucepan of boiling, salted water, cook the broccoli until crisp-tender but still green, 2 to 3 minutes. Remove with a slotted spoon and rinse with cold water.

2. Add the pasta to the boiling water and cook until just done, about 14 minutes. Drain, rinse with cold water, and drain well. Transfer the pasta to a large serving bowl.

3. Add the broccoli, scallions, tomatoes, tuna, garlic, parsley, basil, oil, salt, and pepper to the pasta and toss gently to mix. Serve at room temperature. (Do not refrigerate.)

—EDWARD GIOBBI

CAPELLINI WITH CALAMARI AND SHRIMP

There are two ways to cook calamari: long, slow simmering that makes it melt-ingly tender, or brief cooking of just 1 to 2 minutes to maintain its delicate texture. Anything in between makes the texture rubbery. The quick method is used here—be careful not to overcook the calamari. Chopped walnuts and red-pepper flakes add a delightful dimension to this light pasta-of-the-sea.

WINE RECOMMENDATION
The flavors of this dish are definitely strong enough for a red wine, but make it a low-tannin type, such as a light-bodied Bardolino. Alternatively, a medium-bodied white such as a good Verdicchio would work.

SERVES 4

¼ cup chopped walnuts

¼ cup extra-virgin olive oil

2 large cloves garlic, minced

1½ cups Chicken Stock, page 79, or canned low-sodium chicken broth

1 14-ounce can tomatoes, drained and chopped

¼ cup dry white wine

¼ cup chopped flat-leaf parsley

1½ teaspoons dried oregano

½ teaspoon salt

¼ teaspoon fresh-ground black pepper

¾ pound capellini or angel hair

10 ounces cleaned calamari, bodies cut into thin rings, tentacles cut in half

½ pound large shrimp, shelled, deveined, and cut into thirds

¼ teaspoon dried red-pepper flakes

1. In a small frying pan, toast the walnuts over low heat, stirring frequently, until golden brown, about 5 minutes. Or toast them in a 350° oven for about 8 minutes.

2. In a large stainless-steel frying pan, heat the oil over moderate heat. Add the garlic and cook, stirring occasionally, until it begins to brown, about 2 minutes. Stir in the stock, tomatoes, wine, parsley, oregano, salt, and black pepper. Bring to a boil. Reduce the heat and simmer until the liquid has reduced by half, about 8 minutes.

3. In a large pot of boiling, salted water, cook the pasta just until done, about 3 minutes. Drain.

4. Meanwhile, add the calamari and shrimp to the sauce and simmer until just cooked through, about 2 minutes.

5. Transfer the pasta to a large serving bowl. Add the seafood sauce and toss well. Sprinkle with the red-pepper flakes and toasted walnuts.

—MARK COX, TONY'S, HOUSTON

GARLIC-ANCHOVY PASTA WITH BAKED CALAMARI

Calamari covered with a crunchy mixture of bread crumbs and oregano and briefly baked, then served on a bed of capellini tossed in a pungent anchovy, garlic, and olive oil sauce makes a quick and unusual main course. Any thin dried pasta, such as angel hair or spaghettini, can be substituted for the capellini.

WINE RECOMMENDATION
The flavorful sauce dictates a white wine with fairly intense flavor and a rich, substantial texture. Tocai Friulano is ideal.

SERVES 4

1½ pounds cleaned small calamari bodies cut into ¼-inch rings, tentacles cut in half if large

1 cup dry bread crumbs

1 teaspoon dried oregano

1 teaspoon salt

1 teaspoon fresh-ground black pepper

½ cup plus 2 tablespoons olive oil

1 large clove garlic, minced

1 teaspoon anchovy paste

½ pound capellini or angel hair

1 tablespoon butter

Lemon wedges, for serving

1. Heat the oven to 450°. In a large bowl, toss the calamari with the bread crumbs, oregano, salt, and pepper. Spread the calamari in a large baking dish in a single layer and sprinkle with any crumbs remaining in the bowl. Drizzle 6 tablespoons of the oil on top. Bake until the squid is golden brown and crunchy, about 10 minutes.

2. Meanwhile, in a small saucepan, whisk the garlic and anchovy paste into the remaining ¼ cup oil and bring to a simmer over low heat. Cook, whisking, until the garlic is fragrant but not browned, about 3 minutes.

3. In a large pot of boiling, salted water, cook the capellini until just done, about 3 minutes. Drain the pasta and return it to the pot. Add the anchovy sauce and the butter and toss to coat.

4. Make a bed of capellini on a platter or individual plates. Mound the baked calamari on the pasta and serve with lemon wedges.

—TRACEY SEAMAN

PASTA WITH SMOKED TROUT

Trout are plentiful in the icy rivers and streams that flow through Italy, and they are eaten in many guises. For this dish, smoked trout pieces are added to a simple tomato-cream sauce and served over pasta for a rich and satisfying main course.

WINE RECOMMENDATION
This is definitely not your everyday pasta—and it calls for a wine beyond your everyday white. A fine-quality white wine from the Friuli region, such as Jermann's Vintage Tunina, should be subtle enough to accommodate this dish, yet serious enough to do it justice. Don't serve fine white such as this too cold!

SERVES 4 TO 6

2   whole smoked trout (about ½ pound each)

1   pound penne, ziti, or bow ties

3   tablespoons olive oil or other vegetable oil

2   tablespoons finely chopped shallots

½   pound fresh tomatoes (about 2 small), peeled, seeded, and chopped, or one 14-ounce can tomatoes, drained, pureed, and strained, if desired, to remove the seeds

1   cup half-and-half or light cream

    Dash grated nutmeg

¼   teaspoon salt

½   teaspoon fresh-ground black pepper

¼   cup brandy

    Finely chopped flat-leaf parsley, for garnish

    Grated Parmesan cheese, for garnish

1. Remove the skin from the trout and lift each fillet off the bone. Break the fillets into 1-inch chunks.

2. In a large pot of boiling, salted water, cook the pasta until almost tender, 8 to 10 minutes. Drain.

3. Meanwhile, in a large frying pan, heat the oil. Over low heat add the shallots and cook until soft and translucent, 3 to 5 minutes. Add the tomatoes, cover, and simmer for 5 minutes. Add the half-and-half, nutmeg, salt, and pepper. Cook for 3 minutes.

4. Add the brandy and pasta. Increase the heat to high and cook, tossing frequently, until the pasta is just done and the sauce thickens, 2 to 3 minutes. Add the trout and toss until hot, about 30 seconds. Garnish with parsley and Parmesan.

—EDWARD GIOBBI

Malloreddus with Saffron, Tomato, and Sausage Sauce

Malloreddus are saffron-tinted semolina or cornmeal dumplings, similar to gnocchi, that are unique to Sardinia. Saffron is characteristic of Sardinian cooking. In the sauce it adds a subtly rich flavor, and imparts a deep golden cast to the red of the tomato.

WINE RECOMMENDATION

This sweet, intriguing sauce calls for a flavorful red wine that's low in tannin. A Cannonau from Sardinia, made from the low-tannin grenache grape, is one candidate, as is the always-accommodating barbera.

SERVES 4 TO 6

2½ cups canned tomatoes in puree

1 tablespoon extra-virgin olive oil

1 large red or yellow onion, finely chopped

1 pound mild Italian sausages, casings removed

⅛ teaspoon saffron threads or powder
   Salt

1 pound malloreddus or cavatelli
   Grated Romano cheese, for serving

1. Drain the tomatoes in a strainer set over a medium bowl and reserve the puree. Working over the strainer, scoop out any seeds with your fingers and discard. Coarsely chop the tomatoes and add to the liquid in the bowl.

2. In a large stainless-steel saucepan, heat the oil over moderate heat. Add the onion and cook, stirring occasionally, until softened, about 10 minutes. Add the sausage and cook, stirring occasionally, until browned, about 8 minutes. Add the tomatoes with the juice.

3. In a small frying pan, toast the saffron threads, if using, over low heat for 1 minute. Crush them between your fingers and stir them into the sauce; or stir in the saffron powder. Season the sauce with salt, reduce the heat to moderately low, and simmer, stirring occasionally, until thickened, about 25 minutes.

4. Meanwhile, in a large pot of boiling, salted water, cook the malloreddus according to the package directions until just done. Drain the dumplings and transfer to a large shallow serving bowl. Spoon the sauce over them and toss gently. Serve with the Romano.

—Julia Della Croce

PENNE WITH LAMB RAGU

This is a piquant sauce from the mountainous region of Abruzzo. Only in sauces like this, where the object is to extract as much flavor as possible from a small amount of meat, do Southern Italians cook tomatoes for a long time—and then always gently. You can also use this sauce for lasagne or cannelloni, or with polenta or risotto.

WINE RECOMMENDATION
The meaty flavors of this dish give you license to choose a serious red wine, but you should select one that is not very tannic, lest the acidity of the tomatoes makes it taste astringent. A traditional-style Chianti Classico (one not aged in French oak), a Rosso di Montalcino, or an aged Brunello di Montalcino would be appropriate.

SERVES 4 TO 6

- 3 tablespoons olive oil
- ¾ pound lean boneless lamb shoulder, cut into ½-inch cubes
- 2 cloves garlic, chopped
- ½ teaspoon dried rosemary
- 1 tablespoon chopped flat-leaf parsley
- 1 small dried red chile pepper or ¼ teaspoon dried red-pepper flakes
- ½ teaspoon salt
- ½ cup dry white wine
- 1 35-ounce can tomatoes, well drained and pureed
- 1 pound penne

1. In a large stainless-steel frying pan, heat the oil over high heat. Add the lamb and cook, tossing frequently, until lightly browned, 1 to 2 minutes.

2. Add the garlic, rosemary, parsley, chile pepper, and salt and cook, stirring frequently, for 30 seconds. Pour in the wine and boil, scraping the bottom of the pan to dislodge any browned bits, until slightly reduced, 2 to 3 minutes. Add the tomatoes, cover, and simmer over low heat until the lamb is very tender, about 1½ hours.

3. Meanwhile, in a large pot of boiling, salted water, cook the penne until just done, about 13 minutes. Drain.

4. Remove the chile pepper, if using, from the sauce and toss the pasta with the sauce.

—TOM MARESCA AND DIANE DARROW

CAPELLINI ALLA PROVINCIALE

Now over half a century old, Amerigo's is a great Bronx restaurant that represents the robust and generous cooking of Southern Italy. Capellini alla Provinciale, a specialty, is full of the hearty flavors of the Neapolitan kitchen.

WINE RECOMMENDATION The lusty character of this dish requires an equally lusty wine. Try a bottle of Salice Salentino from the Southern region of Puglia, or another Southern Italian red wine.

SERVES 6 TO 8

1½	cups olive oil
6	large Spanish onions (about 3½ pounds), thinly sliced
4	anchovy fillets, chopped
2	tablespoons chopped fresh parsley
1	tablespoon chopped fresh basil
1	small green bell pepper, thinly sliced
½	cup Gaeta or other oil-cured black olives, pitted and coarsely chopped
¼	cup capers, chopped
2	teaspoons fresh-ground black pepper
10	ounces prosciutto, finely chopped (about 2 cups)
2	cups dry white wine
1	14-ounce can tomatoes, drained and chopped
1	pound capellini or angel hair
	Grated Parmesan cheese, for serving

1. In a large pot, heat the oil over moderate heat. Add the onions, cover, reduce the heat to low, and cook, stirring occasionally, until very soft, about 20 minutes. Uncover, increase the heat to moderate, and cook, stirring occasionally, until the onions are golden brown, about 15 minutes longer.

2. Add the anchovies, parsley, basil, bell pepper, olives, capers, and black pepper. Cook for 30 seconds. Add the prosciutto and wine, bring to a boil over high heat, and boil until most of the liquid has evaporated, about 10 minutes. Add the tomatoes and return to a boil. Reduce the heat to low, cover, and simmer for 30 minutes.

3. In a large pot of boiling, salted water, cook the pasta until just done, about 3 minutes. Drain and return to the pot.

4. Add half the sauce to the pasta and toss to coat. Place the pasta on a large serving platter, pour in the rest of the sauce, and serve with the Parmesan.

—AMERIGO'S, THE BRONX, NEW YORK

Bow Ties with Veal, Lemon, and Pine Nut Sauce

Pine nuts (pignoli) add an interesting texture and a nutty flavor to this meat sauce. The sauce is designed for an inexpensive cut of veal, such as the shoulder, which will stand up to lengthy cooking.

WINE RECOMMENDATION

The simple flavors of this dish enable it to be accompanied by any fresh-tasting, medium-bodied red wine, such as a lighter Chianti or a Rosso di Montalcino. An oaky Italian chardonnay would also be lovely, echoing the lemony accents of the dish.

SERVES 4

4 veal shoulder steaks (about 1 inch thick)

¼ cup flour

2 tablespoons butter

2 tablespoons vegetable oil

½ cup dry white wine

1 tablespoon finely chopped fresh rosemary, or ½ teaspoon dried

  About 2 cups Chicken Stock, page 79, or canned low-sodium chicken broth

2 2-inch strips lemon zest

1 tablespoon pine nuts, coarsely chopped

½ teaspoon salt

¼ teaspoon fresh-ground white or black pepper

¾ pound bow ties

1. Trim any excess fat from the veal steaks and cut each in half. Spread the flour on a sheet of wax paper.

2. In a large deep frying pan, heat 1 tablespoon of the butter with 1 tablespoon of the oil over moderately high heat, until sizzling-hot. Dredge the veal in the flour, shaking off the excess. Add half the meat to the pan and cook, turning once, until brown on both sides, about 15 minutes. Transfer the meat to a platter. Add the remaining 1 tablespoon each butter and oil to the pan and repeat with the remaining meat. Transfer to the platter.

3. Add the wine and rosemary to the pan and cook, stirring, until the wine evaporates, about 1 minute. Stir in ⅓ cup of the stock. Return the veal to the pan in a single layer, cover, reduce the heat to moderately low, and simmer until the stock is absorbed, about 10 minutes. Stir in about ¼ cup more of the stock and cook, adding ¼ cup stock at 10-minute intervals, or as needed to keep the meat moist, for 1 hour.

4. Add the lemon zest. Cover, reduce the heat to low, and cook the veal until tender, about 45 to 60 minutes longer; continue to add stock at 10-minute intervals if necessary. Fifteen minutes before the meat is done, stir in the pine nuts and salt. Transfer the veal to a carving board. Cut

into ¼-inch slices or ½-inch chunks and return to the sauce. Stir in the pepper.

5. Meanwhile, in a large pot of boiling, salted water, cook the pasta until just done, about 9 minutes. Drain the pasta and transfer to a large shallow serving bowl. Spoon the sauce over the pasta and toss gently.

—Julia Della Croce

MAKE IT AHEAD

The sauce can be made up to 3 days ahead. Let cool, cover, and refrigerate. Reheat over low heat, stirring in about ¼ cup additional stock.

GNOCCHI

Like pasta, gnocchi can be eaten as a first course or a side dish, but unlike pasta, they require no special equipment to prepare—not even a rolling pin. Indeed, they are really no more difficult to make than a batch of cookies.

The dough can be formed from a base of potatoes, flour, cornmeal or bread crumbs, and a variety abounds all over Italy. In the Val d'Aosta near Switzerland, for instance, gnocchi are made from buckwheat flour and are served with melted Fontina cheese. Saffron colors the tiny gnocchi of Sardinia, and pumpkin is favored in Lombardy. In the Alto Aldige region, bordering on Austria, gnocchi are made with rye bread crumbs. In the mountainous Abruzzi region, gnocchi are served like spaghetti carbonara, with an egg and pancetta sauce. North of Venice in Friuli, sweet gnocchi, flavored with raisins, cocoa, and cinnamon, are a traditional Christmas treat.

—Michele Scicolone

POTATO GNOCCHI WITH TOMATO SAUCE

Just about every culture has its dumpling, and Italy has gnocchi. These little dumplings range from feathery, light ones made with ricotta to the more substantial potato variety. All these gnocchi need is a simple topping such as tomato sauce, or butter and grated Parmesan.

WINE RECOMMENDATION
If you choose a fresh, light-bodied, crisp Italian white wine, the simple, relatively delicate flavors of this dish can shine through. Lugana or Bianco di Custoza would be an interesting selection. Among red wines, Dolcetto should work.

SERVES 8

3 pounds baking potatoes (about 6)

2 cups flour

4 large eggs, lightly beaten

1 teaspoon salt

¼ teaspoon fresh-ground white pepper

⅛ teaspoon grated nutmeg

1 cup grated Parmesan cheese (about ¼ pound)

Marinara Sauce, page 128, or Creamy Tomato Sauce, page 125

1. Put the potatoes in a pot of salted water. Bring to a boil, reduce the heat, and simmer until tender, about 20 minutes.

2. Drain the potatoes. When cool enough to handle, peel them and work them through a ricer or a food mill into a large bowl. Stir in the flour, eggs, salt, white pepper, nutmeg, and Parmesan until just mixed.

3. Lightly flour a work surface. Divide the dough into 8 pieces. Using your hands, roll each piece into a ½-inch-thick rope. Cut into 1-inch lengths.

4. In a large pot of simmering, salted water, cook one quarter of the gnocchi until they rise to the surface, 3 to 5 minutes. Remove with a slotted spoon and drain in a colander, then transfer to a large warmed serving bowl and cover to keep warm. Cook the remaining gnocchi in three more batches; drain and transfer to the bowl.

5. Meanwhile, reheat the sauce if necessary. Ladle the tomato sauce over the gnocchi and toss until well coated.

—DA CELESTINO, FLORENCE, ITALY

MAKE IT AHEAD

The gnocchi can be made several hours ahead of time. Arrange the uncooked gnocchi on baking sheets in a single layer. Cover and refrigerate.

LASAGNE WITH ROAST CHICKEN AND PORCINI MUSHROOMS

Italians often serve lasagne to commemorate a special occasion or to celebrate a holiday, and this slightly sophisticated version would make a fine entrée for such an event. It is not a difficult recipe, although, like most lasagne, it is time-consuming. Look for pasta sheets at shops that sell freshly cut pasta.

WINE RECOMMENDATION

An earthy red wine such as Chianti would work well with this lasagne. If you want a wine that contrasts with the richness of the dish, choose a light-bodied, simple Chianti; if you want a wine that matches the intensity of the food, choose a Chianti Classico Riserva.

SERVES 6 TO 8

1 chicken (3 to 3½ pounds)
 Salt and fresh-ground black pepper
1 small lemon, halved
1 medium red onion, halved
1 fresh rosemary sprig, or ½ teaspoon dried
⅓ cup plus 3 tablespoons extra-virgin olive oil
1½ ounces dried porcini mushrooms
2 cups boiling water
¼ pound mixed fresh mushrooms such as button, shiitake, and oyster
2 large cloves garlic, chopped
¾ pound spinach, stems removed and leaves washed
2 tablespoons chopped fresh oregano, or ½ teaspoon dried

1 pound fresh mozzarella, cut into ¼-inch dice, plus ¼ pound, shredded
1 pound ricotta cheese (about 2 cups)
1⅓ cups grated Pecorino Romano cheese (about 5 ounces)
½ cup coarsely chopped fresh basil
5 6 by 12-inch sheets fresh pasta
 Marinara Sauce, page 128
2 tablespoons 1-inch-length fresh chives, for garnish

1. Heat the oven to 400°. Sprinkle the cavity of the chicken with ⅛ teaspoon each salt and pepper and stuff with the lemon, onion, and rosemary. Twist the wings behind its back and tie the legs together. Rub the skin with 1 tablespoon of the oil and ⅛ teaspoon each salt and pepper. Put the chicken, breast-side up, on a rack in a roasting pan.

2. Roast the chicken until done, about 1 hour. Transfer the bird to a carving board and let cool slightly, then remove all of the meat, tearing it into 1-inch chunks. Discard the bones, skin, and fat.

3. Put the porcini in a small bowl and pour the boiling water over them. Soak

until softened, about 20 minutes. Remove the mushrooms and squeeze out as much liquid as possible. Coarsely chop. If using shiitake mushrooms, remove the stems. Slice all the fresh mushrooms ¼ inch thick.

4. In a large stainless-steel frying pan, heat ⅓ cup of the oil over moderately high heat until hot, about 2 minutes. Add the fresh mushrooms and the garlic and cook, stirring, until the mushrooms are softened, about 3 minutes. Add the porcini and cook until heated through, about 2 minutes. Add the spinach, reduce the heat to moderate, and cook, stirring, until most of the liquid has evaporated, about 10 minutes. Add the oregano, 1 teaspoon salt, and ½ teaspoon pepper. Remove from the heat and stir in the chicken. Season with additional salt and pepper, if necessary.

5. In a large bowl, combine the diced mozzarella, the ricotta, Romano, and basil.

6. In a large pot of boiling, salted water, cook 1 of the pasta sheets until just done, about 1½ minutes. Using two slotted spoons or spatulas, carefully transfer the sheet to a work surface. Using your fingers, coat each side with a little of the remaining oil to prevent sticking. Repeat with the remaining 4 sheets of pasta.

7. Heat the oven to 350°. Lightly oil the bottom of a 9 by 13-inch glass baking dish. Line the bottom of the dish with a layer of pasta, using one sheet and part of another to cover. Spread half of the cheese mixture over the pasta and cover with another layer of pasta. Spread the mushroom-chicken mixture over the pasta and cover with another layer of pasta. Spread the remaining cheese mixture over the pasta and top with a final layer of pasta. Sprinkle the shredded mozzarella on top.

8. Bake the lasagne until heated through, about 30 minutes. Do not let it bubble, or the cheese will become rubbery.

9. Heat the broiler. Broil the lasagne until the top is browned, about 1 minute. Let rest in a warm spot for 10 minutes before cutting.

10. Meanwhile, reheat the tomato sauce if necessary. Spoon the sauce onto warmed dinner plates. Put the lasagne in the center and garnish with the chives. Pass the remaining sauce separately.

—STEVEN SINGER, SFUZZI

MAKE IT AHEAD

You can assemble the lasagne through step 7 up to a day ahead; cover and refrigerate. Add an additional 10 minutes to the baking time if baking right from the refrigerator.

LASAGNE WITH FOUR CHEESES

This rich lasagne is actually quite simple to make. A basic white sauce (*balsamella*) made with Gruyère, Parmesan, mozzarella, and Pecorino Romano fills the layers and makes the topping. It can be served as a separate pasta course or as a meal in itself with a salad of bitter greens.

WINE RECOMMENDATION
To cut the richness of the cheeses, go for a crisp white wine such as Vernaccia di San Gimignano, or a lighter red wine such as Bardolino or Dolcetto.

SERVES 8 TO 10

½ pound lasagne noodles

4½ tablespoons butter

3 tablespoons flour

1 quart milk, heated

1 cup coarsely grated Swiss Gruyère cheese (about ¼ pound)

1¼ cups grated Parmesan cheese (about 5 ounces)

¾ cup diced mozzarella (about ¼ pound)

1 cup grated Pecorino Romano or Italian Fontina cheese (about ¼ pound)

¾ teaspoon fresh-ground white pepper

1. In a large pot of boiling, salted water, cook the lasagne noodles until just done, 10 to 12 minutes. Drain. Lay the noodles in a single layer on kitchen towels.

2. Heat the oven to 350°. Butter a 9 by 13-inch baking dish.

3. In a large heavy saucepan, melt 3 tablespoons of the butter over moderately low heat. Whisk in the flour and cook, stirring constantly, for 2 to 3 minutes. Gradually whisk in the hot milk, stirring until smooth. Bring to a boil, reduce the heat slightly, and cook, stirring frequently, for 5 minutes. Add the Gruyère, 1 cup of the Parmesan, the mozzarella, and Romano and cook until the cheeses melt, 5 to 7 minutes. Season with the white pepper.

4. Line the bottom of the baking dish with one quarter of the lasagne noodles. Spread one quarter of the cheese sauce over the pasta. Make three more layers of pasta and sauce. Sprinkle the remaining ¼ cup Parmesan over the top and dot with the remaining 1½ tablespoons butter.

5. Bake in the middle of the oven until bubbly and golden brown, 30 to 40 minutes. Let rest in a warm spot for 10 minutes before serving.

—HELEN MILLMAN

CHRISTMAS EVE LASAGNE FROM PIEDMONT

This lasagne is not at all like the many-layered, baked versions of Bologna. Instead, sheets of pasta are simply sauced with butter, anchovies, garlic, and Parmesan cheese. The noodles represent the swaddling clothes that wrapped Baby Jesus in the manger. Fresh lasagne noodles are best, but if you use packaged noodles, cut them in half crosswise and be sure they are sauced very quickly after they are cooked and drained.

WINE RECOMMENDATION
With this simple, rustic dish, choose a white wine with enough flavor to stand up to the anchovies. Arneis, a flavorful white from Piedmont, will do the trick.

SERVES 6

¼ pound butter

8 anchovy fillets, drained and finely chopped

2 large cloves garlic, minced

1 pound lasagne noodles, preferably fresh, cut into 6 by 3½-inch pieces

¼ cup grated Parmesan cheese, plus more for serving

Fresh-ground black pepper

1. In a large saucepan, melt the butter over moderate heat. Add the anchovies and garlic and cook, mashing the anchovies with a spoon, until the garlic is softened but not browned, 3 to 5 minutes.

2. Meanwhile, in a large pot of boiling, salted water, cook the lasagne noodles until just done, about 1 minute for fresh or 10 minutes for dried. Drain immediately and toss in a large bowl with the Parmesan to coat. Quickly transfer the noodles to the anchovy-butter sauce, grind lots of pepper over them, and toss to coat well. Serve with additional Parmesan.

—CAROL FIELD

CHRISTMAS PASTA

Pastas made for Christmas Eve are always without meat (a tradition dating from church vigil days, when Catholics ate only fish on Fridays). But let Christmas Day come, and pastas stuffed with prosciutto and mortadella and cheeses and eggs pour forth. In the north of Italy, *il cenone*, the big dinner, is served on Christmas Eve, while in the south, Christmas Day lunch is a much bigger celebration. In some places, people manage to put away two major meals in less than 24 hours.

—CAROL FIELD

BAKED RIGATONI WITH BRAISED BEEF, OLIVES, AND MOZZARELLA

This dish is inspired by the Italian practice of saucing pasta with leftover pot roast juices as well as by a traditional French dish called *macaronade* (pasta sauced with braised beef juices, which precedes or accompanies the meat). Most of the work for this dish is done a day or so in advance. If you're planning to feed a large crowd, double the recipe. To complete the menu, mix up a green salad, grill a batch of garlic bread, and keep the red wine flowing.

WINE RECOMMENDATION
If you are serving this dish as a main course, choose a hearty red wine such as a Southern Italian red or even a finer wine such as Barolo. If the dish is a first course, however, a lighter-bodied red such as a cabernet from northeastern Italy would be more appropriate.

SERVES 6 TO 8

- 1 2-pound boneless beef chuck or other pot roast
- 1 large onion, sliced
- 1 large carrot, sliced
- 4 cloves garlic, minced
- 1 28-ounce can tomatoes with their juice, crushed
- ½ cup dry red wine
- ½ cup Beef Stock, page 78, or canned low-sodium beef broth
- 2 tablespoons chopped fresh basil
- 2½ teaspoons dried thyme
- 2½ teaspoons dried marjoram
- 2 bay leaves
- ½ teaspoon salt

- 1 pound rigatoni
- 18 Kalamata or other brine-cured black olives, pitted
- ½ cup grated Parmesan cheese
- ½ cup chopped flat-leaf parsley
- 1 pound whole-milk mozzarella, cut into ¼-inch dice, at room temperature
- 1 teaspoon fresh-ground pepper

1. Heat the oven to 350°. Put the roast in a 2½- to 3-quart casserole and surround it with the onion, carrot, and garlic. Add the tomatoes, wine, stock, basil, thyme, marjoram, bay leaves, and salt. Bake, covered, for 1½ hours. Turn the roast and bake until tender, about 1 hour longer. Let the roast cool to room temperature in the braising liquid. Cover and refrigerate overnight.

2. Remove the fat from the surface of the braising liquid. Discard the bay leaves. Transfer the roast to a cutting board. Trim away any surface fat and cut the meat into ¼-inch dice. Stir the diced beef into the braising liquid.

3. In a large pot of boiling, salted water, cook the rigatoni until almost tender but still slightly underdone, 8 to 10 minutes. Drain, rinse with cold water, and drain again.

4. Heat the oven to 375°. Reheat the beef sauce. Stir in the olives, Parmesan, and parsley.

5. In a large bowl, toss the beef sauce, mozzarella, pasta, and pepper. Spoon the pasta into a large baking dish. Bake in the middle of the oven until the top is well browned and the cheese is melted, 40 to 50 minutes.

—MICHAEL MCLAUGHLIN

MAKE IT AHEAD

You can prepare the beef through step 2 up to two days ahead; cover and refrigerate. The pasta can be cooked up to 3 hours ahead; drain and rinse, toss with 2 tablespoons olive oil, cover, and keep at room temperature.

GRATING CHEESES

Grana, which in Italian means "grain," is the generic term for the hard, granular Italian cheeses that were developed around the 13th century in the Po Valley. The oldest and most well known of these cheeses is Parmigiano-Reggiano (known as *grana tìpico* in Italy); others are Asiago, Romano, Lodigiano, Padano, and Piacentino. These cheeses are usually made in thick wheels with a diameter of up to 18 inches.

Although these sharp, flavorful cheeses are often used for grating—over pasta or vegetables, into salads—or for adding to recipes, young *grana* (aged for less than a year) can be served as a table cheese.

CAPPELLETTI IN CAPON BROTH

This filled hat-shaped pasta, similar to but smaller than cappellacci, is traditionally served in capon broth for Christmas lunch in Umbria. Ask your butcher to grind the meat for you, or grind it yourself in a food processor.

WINE RECOMMENDATION
The flavors here are so utterly delicious and complex that you want a wine that doesn't distract you. Any traditional Italian white wine, such as Soave, Orvieto, Frascati, or Trebbiano d'Abruzzo, will work because of its unassertive flavor and high acidity.

SERVES 8

- 3 cups flour
- 1¼ teaspoons salt
- 4 large eggs
- 1 tablespoon butter
- 2½ ounces ground boneless skinless chicken breast
- 1¼ ounces ground lean veal
- 1¼ ounces ground lean pork
- 1 large egg yolk
- ⅓ cup grated Parmesan cheese
- Pinch grated nutmeg
- Pinch ground cinnamon
- 3 quarts Capon Broth, page 120, Chicken Stock, page 79, or canned low-sodium chicken broth
- Grated Parmesan cheese, for serving

1. In a food processor, combine the flour and 1 teaspoon of the salt. Process briefly to mix. With the machine running, add the eggs one at a time and process to form a loose dough. (If the dough isn't quite moist enough, add a few drops of water.) Turn out onto a lightly floured surface and knead until it forms a smooth ball, about 1 minute. Cover with plastic wrap and let rest for at least 20 minutes.

2. In a small frying pan, melt the butter over moderately low heat. Add the chicken, veal, and pork, and cook, stirring occasionally, until the pork is no longer pink, about 10 minutes. Transfer to a medium bowl and let cool.

3. Add the egg yolk, Parmesan, nutmeg, cinnamon, and the remaining ¼ teaspoon salt to the meat and mix well.

4. Divide the dough into pieces the size of a lemon. Roll out each piece through a pasta machine to the thinnest setting. Using a 2-inch cookie cutter, cut the dough into rounds.

5. Spoon ½ teaspoon of the filling onto the center of each round. Moisten the edges lightly with water and fold in half to form a half-moon shape. Pinch the edges firmly together to seal. Shape into little hats by bringing the two pointed ends together,

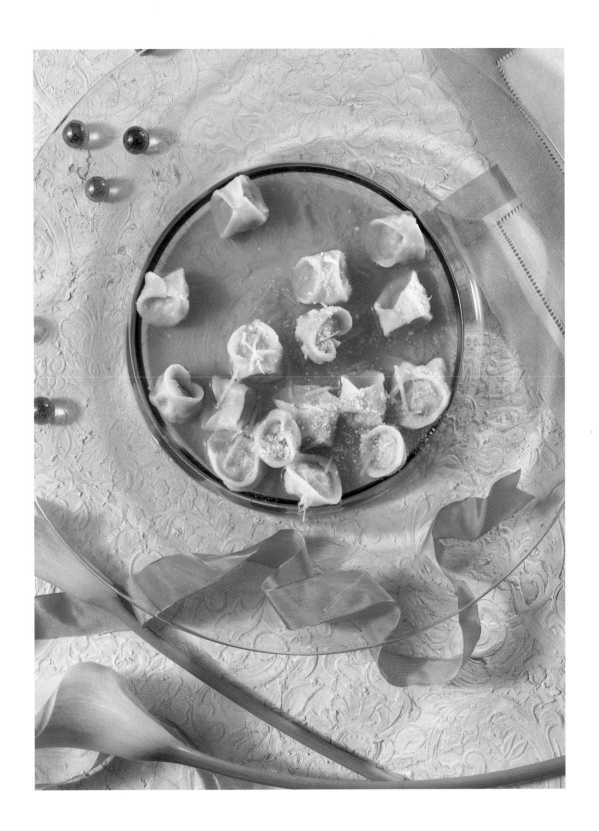

overlapping one on top of the other and pressing them firmly together.

6. In a large saucepan, bring the broth to a boil over high heat. Add the cappelletti and cook until just done, about 5 minutes.

7. Ladle the broth and pasta into soup bowls. Serve with Parmesan on the side.

—CAROL FIELD

MAKE IT AHEAD

You can make the filling up to 2 days ahead; cover and refrigerate. The pasta dough can be made up to a day ahead; cover and refrigerate.

CAPON BROTH

Capon makes a particularly luxurious broth. You can, of course, substitute a stewing hen or roasting chicken.

MAKES ABOUT 6 QUARTS

- 3 carrots, cut into quarters
- 3 ribs celery, coarsely chopped
- 2 onions, cut into quarters
- 6½ quarts water
- 16 to 20 sprigs flat-leaf parsley
- 1 tablespoon salt
- 1 small capon (about 5 pounds)

1. Put all the ingredients in a large pot. Bring to a boil and skim the foam that rises to the surface. Reduce the heat and simmer, uncovered, for 2 hours.

2. Remove the capon and reserve for another use. Strain the broth. Press the vegetables firmly to get all the liquid. Skim the fat from the surface if using the broth immediately. If not, refrigerate for up to a week, or freeze and scrape off the fat before using.

—CAROL FIELD

CHEESE-AND-HERB TORTELLI MARINARA

Tortelli are ravioli with less filling, which creates their signature wide border of dough (called *code*). Sometimes they are made quite large, but these are about 2-inch squares, similar in size to ravioli.

WINE RECOMMENDATION

This dish has delicate flavor, but the tomato sauce is slightly acidic. A lighter-bodied, high-acid red wine, such as a Valtellina wine (Sassella or Inferno), will do the trick.

SERVES 6

4 cups flour

½ teaspoon plus pinch salt

2 large eggs

½ cup lukewarm water

1 pound ricotta cheese (about 2 cups)

½ cup grated Parmesan cheese

1 tablespoon minced fresh basil

1 tablespoon minced flat-leaf parsley

1 clove garlic, minced

¼ teaspoon fresh-ground black pepper

Marinara Sauce, page 128, heated

1. Put the flour and a pinch of salt in a large bowl. Beat 1 of the eggs with the water. Stir into the flour. If the dough is dry, add a little more water by drops. Let the dough rest in the bowl, covered with plastic wrap, for at least 1 hour.

2. In a medium bowl, beat the remaining egg. Add the ricotta, Parmesan, basil, parsley, garlic, ¼ teaspoon salt, and the pepper and beat well. Cover and refrigerate.

3. Divide the dough into 4 pieces. Wrap 3 pieces in plastic and set aside. Cut the piece of dough into 2 smaller pieces. Knead by passing it through a pasta machine at the widest setting two or three times, until it is silky-smooth and no longer sticky. Continue to pass the dough through the pasta machine, moving the setting of the machine to the next notch each time, until the pasta has passed through the thinnest setting.

4. Put the sheets of pasta on a well-floured work surface. Spoon generous ½ teaspoonfuls of the cheese filling, 1½ inches apart in straight rows, along the sheets. Brush the exposed areas of dough lightly with water. Drape the second sheet of dough on top and with your fingers press lightly around each mound of filling. With a sharp knife or fluted pastry wheel, cut the tortelli into 2-inch squares. Repeat with the remaining dough and filling.

5. In a large pot of boiling, salted water, cook the tortelli in batches until just done, about 6 minutes. Remove with a slotted spoon, drain well, and transfer to a serving bowl. Spoon on a little sauce to prevent them from sticking. Pour the remaining sauce over the tortelli and serve.

—FRED FERRETTI

CAPPELLACCI OF PUMPKIN

The name for this stuffed pasta comes from its shape, which resembles the hats the Alpine climbers wear. In the province of Ferrara, cappellacci are always filled with pumpkin and served as a first course for Christmas Eve dinner. You could also use butternut squash, available year-round.

WINE RECOMMENDATION With the sweet squash flavor of this dish, you can choose either a traditional Italian white wine, whose acidity will counterbalance the squash, or a fuller-bodied white wine, whose richness will match the dish. In the latter category, a new-style Italian white wine that has been aged in French oak would be a good choice.

SERVES 8

- 4 cups unbleached flour
- 2 teaspoons salt
- 5 extra-large eggs
- 2½ pounds pumpkin or butternut squash, cut into large chunks and seeded
- ½ pound butter, ¼ pound cut up and at room temperature, ¼ pound melted
- 1 extra-large egg yolk

  About ⅓ cup grated Parmesan cheese, plus more for serving
- ¼ teaspoon grated nutmeg
- ¼ teaspoon fresh-ground black pepper

1. In a food processor, combine the flour and 1 teaspoon of the salt. Process briefly to mix. With the machine running, add the whole eggs one at a time and process to form a soft dough. (If the dough isn't quite moist enough, add a few drops of water.) Turn out onto a lightly floured surface and knead until it forms a smooth ball, about 1 minute. Cover with plastic wrap and let rest for at least 20 minutes.

2. Heat the oven to 350°. Lightly grease a baking sheet. Put the pumpkin on the baking sheet and bake until tender, 30 to 45 minutes. Let cool, then remove and discard the skin. Work the pumpkin flesh through a ricer or a coarse sieve, or puree in a food processor.

3. Transfer the puree to a bowl. Add the softened butter, the egg yolk, ⅓ cup Parmesan, the nutmeg, the remaining 1 teaspoon salt, and the pepper. Mix until the filling is firm and holds together well. If it is too soft, add a little more Parmesan.

4. Divide the dough into pieces the size of a lemon. Roll out each piece through a pasta machine set to the next-to-the-thinnest setting. Put the sheets of pasta on a well-floured work surface and, using a 3-inch cookie cutter, cut into rounds. Keep the dough you are not working with under plastic wrap or a towel.

5. Spoon a heaping teaspoon of pumpkin filling into the center of each round.

Moisten the edge of each pasta circle lightly with water and fold in half to form a half-moon shape. Press to seal the edges firmly. Shape into little hats by bringing the two pointed ends together, overlapping one on top of the other and pressing them firmly together. If you are not going to use the cappellacci immediately, arrange on a baking sheet lined with parchment paper, cover with plastic wrap, and set aside at room temperature for up to 1 hour. Or refrigerate to hold longer.

6. In a large pot of boiling, salted water, cook the cappellacci until they float to the surface, about 5 minutes. Be careful not to overcook, or the filling will ooze out. Drain and rinse. Transfer the cappellacci to a warm serving dish. Pour the melted butter over the top, sprinkle with Parmesan, and toss gently. Serve with additional Parmesan.

—CAROL FIELD

MAKE IT AHEAD

The dough for the cappellacci can be wrapped in plastic and refrigerated for up to 1 day. Or freeze for up to 2 weeks.

FESTIVE PASTAS

Italians eat pasta all year round—stuffed pasta, dried pasta, fresh egg pasta. And then at Christmas-time, each town and village, each city and *paése* has its own special pasta dish. This may be the one time of year that these festive pastas appear on the table. If this is Mantua, it must be agnolini; and if it's Ferrara, it's pumpkin-filled cappellacci. It's not Christmas in Gubbio, the quaint medieval city north of Perugia, unless there are hat-shaped cappelletti floating in rich broth.

—CAROL FIELD

POTATO, ONION, AND CHEESE RAVIOLI

In Parma, potato ravioli are a traditional treat made with a copious amount of Parmigiano Reggiano. For this filling, we cut down on the Parmesan and added farmer cheese and an onion puree. These ravioli are good with Creamy Tomato Sauce, page 125, or you could use a béchamel sauce made with cheese.

WINE RECOMMENDATION
The type of wine you choose for this hearty dish depends on the sauce. With a red sauce, go for a low-tannin Italian red wine such as Valpolicella or a young Chianti; with a white sauce, try a white wine that has good backbone, such as a better pinot grigio.

MAKES ABOUT 6 DOZEN 2-INCH RAVIOLI

- 2 baking potatoes (about 1 pound in all), peeled and quartered
- 1 tablespoon olive oil
- 2 onions, chopped
- ½ cup grated Parmesan cheese
- ½ pound farmer cheese
- 1 large egg
- 1¼ teaspoons salt
- ¼ teaspoon fresh-ground white pepper
- ¼ teaspoon grated nutmeg
  Fresh Pasta, page 129
  Creamy Tomato Sauce, page 125

1. Put the potatoes in a medium saucepan of salted water. Bring to a boil, reduce the heat, and simmer until tender, about 20 minutes. Drain the potatoes, then work them through a ricer or a food mill into a large bowl.

2. Meanwhile, in a medium frying pan, heat the oil over moderate heat. Add the onions and cook, stirring occasionally, until translucent, about 5 minutes. Put the onions in a food processor and puree.

3. In the large bowl, combine the potatoes, onions, Parmesan, farmer cheese, egg, salt, pepper, and nutmeg. Mix until well blended.

4. Divide the pasta dough into 6 pieces. Working with one piece at a time, pat the dough into a rectangle roughly 6 by 4 inches. Knead by passing it through a pasta machine at the widest setting two or three times, until it is silky-smooth and no longer sticky. Continue to pass the dough through the pasta machine, moving the setting of the machine to the next notch each time, until the pasta has passed through the thinnest setting.

5. Cut each band of dough into two even lengths. Lay one strip of dough on a floured work surface. Spoon or pipe mounds (about 1½ teaspoons) of filling onto the dough, about ½ inch in from the edges and spaced about 1½ inches apart.

6. Brush the exposed areas of dough lightly with water. Drape the second strip of dough on top and, with your fingers, press around each mound of filling and seal the edges. With a sharp knife, fluted pastry wheel, or ravioli stamp, cut the ravioli into 2-inch squares. Repeat with the remaining dough and filling.

7. Reheat the sauce if necessary. In a large pot of boiling, salted water, cook the ravioli, 12 at a time, until just done, 6 to 7 minutes. (Do not overcrowd, or the ravioli may stick together.) Remove with a slotted spoon, drain well, and transfer to a serving bowl. Spoon a little sauce over the ravioli to prevent them from sticking and cover to keep warm while you cook the remaining ravioli. Pour the remaining sauce over the ravioli and serve.

—John Robert Massie

Creamy Tomato Sauce

MAKES ABOUT 1½ CUPS

1 35-ounce can tomatoes with their juice

Bouquet garni: 5 sprigs fresh parsley, ½ teaspoon dried thyme, and 5 peppercorns

¾ cup heavy cream

Salt and fresh-ground black pepper

1. Put the tomatoes in a food processor or blender and puree. Strain the puree.

2. Transfer the puree to a large stainless-steel frying pan. Add the bouquet garni and bring to a boil over moderate heat. Boil, uncovered, until slightly reduced, about 5 minutes. Stir in the cream. Discard the bouquet garni. Season with salt if necessary and pepper to taste.

—John Robert Massie

SPINACH AND RICOTTA RAVIOLI

These ravioli, filled with spinach and ricotta, are a specialty of Northern Italy, but different versions are found throughout the country. They can be served with Marinara Sauce, page 128, or simply with melted butter, grated Parmesan, and fresh-ground black pepper.

WINE RECOMMENDATION
These delicious ravioli call for a white wine. Select a wine that is not oaky but that does have lots of character, such as a good Soave.

MAKES ABOUT 6 DOZEN 2-INCH RAVIOLI

1½ pounds spinach, stems removed and leaves washed, or 1½ packages (15 ounces in all) frozen spinach

1 10-ounce container whole-milk ricotta cheese

1 cup grated Parmesan cheese (about ¼ pound)

2 large eggs

1 teaspoon salt

⅛ teaspoon fresh-ground black pepper

¼ teaspoon grated nutmeg

Fresh Pasta, page 129

Marinara Sauce, page 128

1. If using fresh spinach, steam it over boiling water until wilted and tender but still bright green, 2 to 3 minutes. If using frozen, cook as directed on the package. Drain and rinse with cold water until cooled. Squeeze the spinach by handfuls to remove as much water as possible.

2. Put the spinach in a food processor. Add the ricotta, Parmesan, eggs, salt, pepper, and nutmeg. Process until the spinach is finely chopped and the mixture is smooth, about 1 minute.

3. Divide the pasta dough into 6 pieces. Working with one piece at a time, pat the dough into a rectangle roughly 6 by 4 inches. Knead by passing it through a pasta machine at the widest setting two or three times, until it is silky smooth and no longer sticky. Continue to pass the dough through the pasta machine, moving the setting of the pasta machine to the next notch each time, until the pasta has passed through the thinnest setting.

4. Cut each band of dough into two even lengths. Lay one strip of dough on a floured work surface. Spoon or pipe mounds (about 1½ teaspoons) of filling onto the strip of dough, about ½ inch in from the edges and spaced about 1½ inches apart.

5. Brush the exposed areas of dough lightly with water. Drape the second strip of dough on top and, with your fingers, press around each mound of filling and seal the

edges. With a sharp knife, fluted pastry wheel, or ravioli stamp, cut the ravioli into 2-inch squares.

6. Reheat the sauce if necessary. In a large pot of boiling, salted water, cook the ravioli, 12 at a time, until just done, 6 to 7 minutes. (Do not overcrowd, or the ravioli may stick together.) Remove with a slotted spoon, drain well, and transfer to a serving bowl. Spoon a little sauce over them to prevent them from sticking and cover to keep warm while you cook the remaining ravioli. Pour the remaining sauce over the ravioli and serve.

—JOHN ROBERT MASSIE

MARINARA SAUCE

MAKES ABOUT 3 CUPS

¼ cup extra-virgin olive oil

2 small cloves garlic, minced or crushed (see Note)

2½ pounds plum tomatoes, peeled, seeded, and finely chopped, or one 35-ounce and one 14-ounce can plum tomatoes, drained and chopped

¼ teaspoon salt

½ teaspoon fresh-ground black pepper

2 tablespoons shredded fresh basil

1. In a large stainless-steel saucepan or deep frying pan, heat the oil over moderately low heat. Add the garlic and cook, stirring, until golden, about 4 minutes. Discard the garlic if desired.

2. Add the tomatoes, salt, and pepper. Cook, stirring occasionally, until thickened, about 30 minutes. Soft bits of tomato will remain, and the sauce should be thick enough to hold its shape on a spoon. Stir in the basil just before serving.

NOTE: Crushed garlic cloves can be discarded after browning for a very subtle flavor or left in and discarded at the end of cooking for a slightly more emphatic garlic taste.

—NANCY VERDE BARR

FRESH PASTA

Fresh homemade pasta dough is made with eggs, which add moisture and make the dough soft and easy to work with. The dough can be flavored with fresh herbs, such as basil, chives, or chervil, or grated lemon zest.

MAKES 1¼ TO 1½ POUNDS

About 2½ cups all-purpose or bread flour

3 large eggs

1 large egg yolk

2 teaspoons olive oil

Pinch salt

1. Put 2½ cups flour in a medium bowl. Make a well in the center and add the eggs, egg yolk, oil, and salt. Using a fork or your fingers, blend the ingredients in the well. Gradually work in the flour until the dough masses together and pulls away from the sides of the bowl. It should be soft, pliable, and slightly sticky. If the dough is too stiff and dry, add up to 2 tablespoons of water, 1 teaspoon at a time; if it is too wet and sticky, add flour, 1 tablespoon at a time.

2. Turn the dough out onto a lightly floured surface and knead until smooth and elastic, 8 to 10 minutes.

3. Shape the dough into a ball, dust lightly with flour, and cover with plastic wrap. Let rest for at least 30 minutes before rolling out.

Food Processor Method: In a small bowl, combine the eggs, egg yolk, oil, salt, and 2 tablespoons of water. Put 2½ cups flour in the food processor. With the machine running, pour the egg mixture through the feed tube and process for 10 seconds. The mixture will resemble crumbly meal after 5 seconds and should form a ball after another 5 seconds. If the dough is still crumbly after 10 seconds, add another tablespoon or two of water. Once a ball has formed, transfer the dough to a lightly floured work surface and knead it briefly until smooth and elastic. Shape the dough into a ball, cover with plastic wrap, and let rest for at least 30 minutes before rolling out.

—JOHN ROBERT MASSIE

MAIN COURSES

Tuscan Roast Loin of Pork, page 155

OSSOBUCO WITH GREMOLATA

These fork-tender veal shanks are slowly braised with wine, vegetables, and herbs. They are finished with a garnish of *gremolata*, a mixture of grated lemon zest, chopped parsley, and garlic that adds a welcome piquancy to this rich, meaty dish. Risotto alla Milanese, page 71, is the traditional accompaniment, but lightly buttered fettuccine would be nice too.

WINE RECOMMENDATION

An earthy Italian red wine such as a Chianti Classico or a Vino Nobile di Montepulciano will echo the simple, earthy flavors of this dish, yet stand up to the piquancy of the sauce.

SERVES 8

- 2 tablespoons butter
- 2 tablespoons olive oil
- 5 pounds veal shanks, cut 2 inches thick, tied with string around their circumference
- 1 cup all-purpose flour
- 2 onions, coarsely chopped
- 1 large carrot, coarsely chopped
- 1 rib celery, coarsely chopped
- 3 cloves garlic, crushed
- ½ teaspoon dried marjoram
- ½ teaspoon dried basil
- ½ teaspoon dried thyme
- 1 28-ounce can tomatoes, drained and coarsely chopped
- 2½ tablespoons tomato paste
- 2 cups dry white wine or dry vermouth
- 1 cup Chicken Stock, page 79, or canned low-sodium chicken broth
- 3 strips lemon zest, about 2 inches long
- 1 large bay leaf
- 4 sprigs fresh parsley

Gremolata
- ½ cup minced fresh parsley
- 3 clove garlic, minced
- 1 tablespoon grated lemon zest

1. In a large pot, melt the butter with the oil over moderate heat.

2. Dredge the veal in the flour and shake off any excess. Working in batches, brown the veal on all sides. Do not crowd the pan. Remove to a bowl.

3. Add the onions, carrot, celery, and garlic to the pot, cover, and cook until the vegetables are tender, about 15 minutes.

4. Put the veal on top of the vegetables, making sure the bones are upright. Sprinkle the marjoram, basil, and thyme on top. Add the tomatoes, tomato paste, wine, stock, strips of lemon zest, bay leaf, and parsley sprigs. If necessary, add enough water to cover the shanks.

5. Bring to a boil, reduce the heat to low, and simmer, covered, until the meat is tender, about 2 hours.

6. Transfer the veal shanks to a heated platter; remove the strings and cover with foil to keep warm. Increase the heat under the pot to high and boil, stirring frequently, until the sauce is reduced by half, about 20 minutes. Pour the sauce over the meat.

7. Meanwhile, make the gremolata. In a small bowl, combine the parsley, garlic, and lemon zest. Sprinkle it over the meat.

—W. Peter Prestcott

Make It Ahead

You can braise the veal shanks up to 3 days ahead. Let cool; cover and refrigerate. Reheat before proceeding with step 6.

SAGE-AND-PEPPER-RUBBED VEAL ROAST

Boneless veal shoulder rubbed with sautéed fresh sage and black pepper makes a comforting roast to serve with sautéed broccoli rabe and roasted potatoes on a chilly evening. The recipe calls for rubbing the outside of the roast with the sage mixture, but you could also unroll the veal and rub some of the mixture over the inside; reroll the meat and tie it, then rub the remaining mixture over the outside of the roast.

WINE RECOMMENDATION
A full-bodied white wine, such as one of the modernistic oaky Italian white wines, would be lovely with this dish. If red is your preference instead, try a Dolcetto, whose black-pepper aroma and taste will echo the dish's flavor.

SERVES 4

2 tablespoons butter

2 tablespoons chopped fresh sage

1 teaspoon fresh-ground black pepper

1 2-pound, boneless veal shoulder roast, rolled and tied

1 tablespoon olive oil

1. Heat the oven to 450°. In a small saucepan, melt the butter over moderate heat. Add the sage and pepper and cook, stirring occasionally, for 1 minute. Let cool slightly, then rub the mixture all over the meat.

2. In a small roasting pan, heat the oil in the oven. Put the veal in the roasting pan and roast for 15 minutes. Turn the meat over and roast for 15 minutes more. Turn the veal again and roast until nicely browned and an instant-read thermometer inserted in the center registers 140°, about 15 minutes longer.

3. Transfer the roast to a carving board, cover with foil, and let stand in a warm spot for 5 minutes before cutting into ⅓-inch slices.

—BOB CHAMBERS

135

SALTIMBOCCA ALLA ROMANO

In this classic Roman dish, veal scallops, sage, and prosciutto often are rolled into sausagelike bundles. In this version, the scallops are left flat. You can substitute turkey breast for the veal with very nice results.

WINE RECOMMENDATION
If a red wine is to accompany this dish, it must be very light, because the dish is elegantly simple. A better Italian white wine, such as a good pinot grigio or other good, unoaked northeastern white, is a surer bet.

SERVES 4

8 veal scaloppine (about 1 pound), pounded ⅛ inch thick

8 fresh sage leaves

8 thin slices prosciutto (about ¼ pound), trimmed to the same size as the scaloppine

⅓ cup flour

1 tablespoon butter

1 tablespoon olive oil

⅓ cup dry white wine

1. Lay the scaloppine on a work surface. Put 1 sage leaf on each slice, cover with a slice of prosciutto, and secure with a toothpick, threading it through the veal so the pick lays flat. Dredge the veal lightly with flour, shaking off the excess.

2. In a large frying pan, melt 1½ teaspoons of the butter with 1½ teaspoons of the oil over moderate heat. Add half the scaloppine and cook, turning once, until lightly browned, 1 to 2 minutes per side. Transfer the veal to a large serving platter. Add the remaining 1½ teaspoons each oil and butter to the pan and repeat with the remaining veal. Transfer to the platter and set aside in a warm spot.

3. Add the wine to the pan and cook, scraping the bottom of the pan to dislodge any browned bits, until it has reduced by half. Pour the pan sauce over the veal and serve.

—Trattoria Pasqualino, Rome

VEAL AND LINGUINE ALLA PIZZAIOLA

Pizzaiola is a dish appreciated in many parts of Italy, but none more so than Naples, where it is made with either veal or beef. Oregano is one of the essential ingredients. Wild oregano is used in Italy, but it's hard to come by here. You can use imported Italian or Greek dried oregano with good results. Serve this dish with an antipasto of mushrooms and a salad of Italian greens for a first course.

WINE RECOMMENDATION
A ripe and flavorful Italian red wine will match the frank flavors of this dish. Many such reds hail from Southern Italy and Sicily—for example Salice Salentino, Corvo, or Regaleali would work well.

SERVES 4

1⅛ tablespoons extra-virgin olive oil

¾ pound veal scaloppine, pounded ⅛ inch thick

Salt and fresh-ground black pepper

2 large cloves garlic, minced

½ cup dry white wine

2 cups canned crushed tomatoes with their liquid

½ cup water

2 tablespoons coarsely chopped flat-leaf parsley

½ teaspoon dried oregano

¾ pound linguine

1. In a large frying pan, preferably non-stick, heat the oil over moderately high heat. Season the veal with salt and pepper and add to the pan in a single layer. Cook until browned, about 2 minutes. Turn the veal, scatter the garlic around it, and cook until the scaloppine are browned, about 2 minutes longer. Transfer the veal to a plate.

2. Add the wine to the pan, bring to a boil, and boil until reduced to 2 tablespoons, about 3 minutes. Stir in the tomatoes, water, parsley, and oregano and season with salt and pepper. Reduce the heat to moderately low and bring to a simmer. Return the veal to the pan and cook, stirring occasionally, until the sauce is thickened and the veal is tender, about 15 minutes.

3. Meanwhile, in a large pot of boiling, salted water, cook the linguine until just done, about 6 minutes. Drain the pasta and transfer to a large bowl. Spoon the tomato sauce over the pasta and toss well. Transfer to plates and serve the veal alongside.

—MICHELE SCICOLONE

VEAL CROQUETTES WITH LEMON

These light croquettes are tender and delicate. Before cooking, the meat mixture is quite soft, so don't be alarmed when you are forming the croquettes. As they bake, the lemon and butter form a light, piquant sauce. Serve the veal croquettes with pan-roasted potatoes and steamed asparagus, and finish with a dessert of fresh ricotta with honey, berries, and biscotti.

WINE RECOMMENDATION

This delicate dish could easily be overwhelmed by an oaky white wine like chardonnay. Instead, try an unoaked Italian white wine, such as a sauvignon or pinot grigio from the region of Friuli or from Trentino-Alto Adige.

SERVES 4 TO 6

12	slices white bread, crusts removed
2	cups milk
¾	pound ground lean veal shoulder
4	large eggs
1	cup grated Parmesan cheese (about ¼ pound)
¼	cup lemon juice
¼	teaspoon salt
½	teaspoon fresh-ground black pepper
4	cups vegetable oil
1½	cups all-purpose flour
4	tablespoons cold butter, cut into pieces

1. In a medium bowl, soak the bread in the milk for 30 minutes.

2. Squeeze the bread as dry as possible and put it into a large bowl; discard the milk. Add the ground veal, eggs, Parmesan, 2 tablespoons of the lemon juice, the salt, and pepper. Mix with a wooden spoon until well blended.

3. Heat the oven to 300°. In a large deep frying pan or deep fryer, heat the oil over moderate heat to 375°.

4. Meanwhile, form the veal mixture into egg-shaped croquettes, using ¼ cup of the mixture for each; the mixture will be quite soft. Lightly dredge the croquettes in the flour and fry in batches, turning once, until golden, about 5 minutes. Transfer to paper towels to drain.

5. Arrange the croquettes in a single layer in a shallow roasting pan. Dot the tops with the butter and drizzle on the remaining 2 tablespoons lemon juice. Bake until heated through, 10 minutes. Serve with the pan juices spooned over the top.

—GIULIANO BUGIALLI

Sauteed Calf's Liver and Onions

Venice produces many versions of this classic combination of calf's liver and onions, but the underlying principle of all of them is the better the liver, the less you have to do with it.

The wine you pair with this dish must match the liver in flavor intensity and the onions in their slightly sweet taste. A richly flavored Amarone della Valpolicella, brimming with ripe fruit, can handle both challenges.

SERVES 4

1   pound calf's liver, thinly sliced and cut into ½-inch-wide strips

1   cup milk

3   tablespoons butter

3   tablespoons olive oil

1   pound sweet onions, such as Bermudas or Vidalias, thinly sliced

½   teaspoon salt

¼   teaspoon fresh-ground black pepper

2   tablespoons minced fresh parsley

Lemon wedges, for garnish

1. Put the liver into a large shallow bowl or glass pie pan. Pour over the milk, cover, and refrigerate for 1 to 3 hours.

2. In a large frying pan, melt the butter with the oil over low heat. Add the onions and cook, stirring occasionally, until very soft and light golden, about 30 minutes.

3. Drain the liver, pat dry, and add to the pan. Increase the heat to moderately high and cook, stirring constantly, until the liver is browned but still rosy inside, about 3 minutes. Add the salt, pepper, and parsley and toss to combine. Serve garnished with the lemon wedges.

—Tom Maresca and Diane Darrow

TUSCAN ROAST LOIN OF PORK

The herb-scented roast loin of pork called *arista* is a classic Tuscan meat dish, most often cooked on a spit over an open wood fire. The fact that this handsome roast is just as good warm or cool as hot (some say it's even better the second day) makes it an ideal dinner-party choice.

WINE RECOMMENDATION
The herbal flavors of this dish beg for a wine with herbal or spicy accents. Try a Barbaresco from the Piedmont region, or a syrah-based Italian wine—it's a grape that some of Italy's best wineries are having good success with.

SERVES 6 TO 8

15 cloves garlic

½ cup fresh rosemary leaves, or 3 tablespoons dried

2 tablespoons salt

1½ tablespoons fresh-ground black pepper

2 tablespoons olive oil

1 5-pound bone-in pork loin

1. In a food processor or blender, chop the garlic and rosemary with the salt and pepper. With the machine running, drizzle in the oil. Process to a thick paste.

2. Put the meat, bone-side down, on a rack in a roasting pan. Rub the herb paste all over the meat. Let sit at cool room temperature for 1 hour.

3. Heat the oven to 325°. Roast the pork loin until the internal temperature reaches 150°, about 1½ hours. Increase the heat to 400° and roast until lightly browned, 10 to 15 minutes longer.

4. Transfer the roast to a carving board. Loosely cover with aluminum foil and let rest in a warm spot for 20 to 30 minutes before carving.

—TOM MARESCA AND DIANE DARROW

CHICKEN BREASTS WITH FENNEL SAUCE

Arrange the slices of chicken in the center of a large platter, slightly overlapping, and surround them with Spinach with Raisins and Pine Nuts, page 250. Pass any extra fennel sauce in a small bowl and let guests serve themselves.

WINE RECOMMENDATION
Delicate egg, earthy porcini, gentle fennel—the flavors of this dish run the gamut, giving you a lot of leeway in selecting a wine. A light-bodied red such as an inexpensive sangiovese would be interesting, as would a medium-bodied white such as a better pinot grigio from Alto Adige.

SERVES 6 TO 8

- 1 ounce dried porcini mushrooms
- 3 large eggs
- 1 tablespoon chopped fresh sage
- ¼ cup grated Parmesan cheese
- 1 teaspoon grated lemon zest
  Salt and fresh-ground black pepper
- 5 tablespoons butter
- 2 whole boneless, skinless chicken breasts (¾ pound each), lightly pounded to an even thickness
- ½ pound mild Italian sausage, casings removed
- 1 cup dry white wine
- 2 fennel bulbs (about 1 pound in all), trimmed and cut into 1-inch pieces
- 1 cup water

1. Put the porcini in a small bowl and pour boiling water to cover over them. Soak until softened, about 20 minutes. Remove the mushrooms and squeeze to remove as much liquid as possible; pat dry.

2. In a small bowl, using a fork, beat the eggs with the sage, Parmesan, lemon zest, and a pinch each of salt and pepper.

3. In a 7-inch skillet, preferably nonstick, melt 1½ teaspoons of the butter over moderate heat. Pour in half of the egg mixture and cook as you would a pancake, until firm, 1 to 2 minutes per side. Transfer to a large plate and repeat with another 1½ teaspoons butter and the remaining egg mixture. Let the omelets cool slightly.

4. Lay the chicken breasts skinned-side down on a work surface. Spread the sausage meat over the chicken and sprinkle the porcini on top; press the mushrooms into the sausage. Lay the omelets on the mushrooms and roll up each chicken breast from one side to the other. Tie the rolled chicken with kitchen string to secure.

5. In a heavy medium pot, melt 2 tablespoons of the butter over high heat. Add

the chicken rolls and cook, turning, until golden brown on all sides, 6 to 8 minutes. Add the wine, a pinch of salt, and ¼ teaspoon pepper. Cover, reduce the heat to low, and simmer, turning occasionally, until the chicken is cooked through, about 30 minutes.

6. Meanwhile, in a large heavy saucepan, melt the remaining 2 tablespoons butter over low heat. Add the fennel, water, and a pinch each of salt and pepper. Cover and cook, stirring occasionally, until the fennel is tender, about 20 minutes. Transfer the fennel and its cooking liquid to a food processor or blender and puree until smooth.

7. Transfer the chicken rolls to a cutting board and remove the strings. Stir the fennel puree into the juices in the pot and bring to a simmer; if the sauce is too thick to pour, add a little water to thin it. Season with salt and pepper.

8. Cut the chicken rolls into ½-inch slices and place on a platter. Strain the fennel sauce over the chicken and serve the extra sauce on the side.

—LORENZA DE'MEDICI

COUNTRY-STYLE FRIED CHICKEN

This simple, succulent chicken dish is a favorite of cookbook author Giuliano Bugialli, who remembers it from his childhood days in the Italian countryside. The secret to the dish is to marinate the chicken in beaten eggs before frying it, resulting in meltingly tender meat.

WINE RECOMMENDATION
This dish is so very simple that it can swing either way with wine, red or white. A fuller-bodied Italian chardonnay or a light-bodied red wine such as an inexpensive Tuscan sangiovese would work equally well.

SERVES 4 TO 6

- 1   teaspoon coarse salt
- 1   chicken (about 3 to 3½ pounds)
      Salt and fresh-ground black pepper
- 1   cup all-purpose flour
- 3   large eggs
- 4   cups vegetable oil
- ½   cup olive oil
- 1   lemon, cut in wedges

1. Bring a large pot of water to a boil over high heat. Add the chicken and salt and boil for 1 minute. Drain well and let cool.

2. Cut the chicken into 8 pieces. Season with 1 teaspoon salt and ½ teaspoon pepper. Dredge in the flour, shaking off the excess. In a large bowl, beat the eggs lightly with a pinch of salt. Add the chicken pieces and turn to coat evenly. Cover and refrigerate for at least 1 hour and up to 2 hours, turning occasionally.

3. Heat the oven to 200°. In a large heavy frying pan, preferably cast iron, heat the vegetable and olive oils over moderate heat to 375°. Add half of the chicken and increase the heat to high for 20 seconds. Reduce the heat to moderate and fry, turning occasionally, until the chicken is golden and crisp and just done, about 25 minutes.

4. Using tongs, transfer the chicken to paper towels to drain. Keep warm in the oven. Fry the remaining chicken. Serve hot, sprinkled with salt and garnished with the lemon wedges.

—GIULIANO BUGIALLI

BABY CLAMS, LIVORNO-STYLE

As with many ports, the cooking of Livorno reflects outside influences and employs the widest range of spices and flavorings of any town in Tuscany. The town is especially known for its spicy dishes made with an abundance of dried red-pepper flakes. The wonderful tiny Mediterranean clams are almost always served in the shell, even when combined with pasta or, as in this dish, with eggs.

WINE RECOMMENDATION

If you like this dish on the spicy side, you'll welcome the softness of a chilled bottle of Gavi, made in the Piedmont region not far from the Tuscan town of Livorno.

SERVES 6

2   pounds small clams, such as littlenecks or razor clams, scrubbed

1   lemon, halved

¼   teaspoon coarse salt

½   cup olive oil

1   small red onion, finely chopped

1   large clove garlic, minced

1   pound plum tomatoes (about 5), peeled, seeded, and cut into chunks, or one 28-ounce can tomatoes, drained, seeded, and cut into chunks

   Salt and fresh-ground black pepper

   About ¼ teaspoon dried red-pepper flakes

2   large eggs

¼   cup coarsely chopped flat-leaf parsley

1. Discard any clams that have broken shells or that do not clamp shut when tapped. Put the clams in a bowl of cold water to cover. Add the lemon and coarse salt and let soak for 30 minutes.

2. In a large frying pan, heat the oil over moderate heat. Add the onion and garlic and cook, stirring occasionally, until slightly softened, 2 to 3 minutes.

3. Add the tomatoes, reduce the heat to low, and cook for 5 minutes, stirring occasionally. Season with salt, black pepper, and the red-pepper flakes.

4. Drain the clams and rinse well with cold water. Add to the pan, cover, and increase the heat to moderately high. Cook, stirring occasionally, just until the clams open, about 3 minutes. Discard any clams that do not open.

5. Meanwhile, in a medium bowl, lightly beat the eggs with a pinch of salt.

6. Remove the frying pan from the heat. Sprinkle the parsley over the clams, pour in the eggs, and mix well until thoroughly blended. Return the pan to moderate heat and cook, stirring frequently, just until hot. Serve immediately.

—GIULIANO BUGIALLI

SPICY CLAM ROAST WITH SAUSAGE AND FENNEL

George Germon and Johanne Killeen are known for their inventive, hearty dishes, such as this one from their restaurant Al Forno, in Providence.

WINE RECOMMENDATION
Such a flavorful, unusual dish as this will dominate most Italian white wines—and what's wrong with that? Serve a simple, earthy, thirst-quenching white wine like a Soave that refreshes the mouth between bites of food but doesn't try to compete.

SERVES 6

- ½ pound hot Italian sausage
- ½ pound chorizo or other spicy sausage
- 4 tablespoons butter
- 2 onions, thinly sliced
- 1 large fennel bulb, thinly sliced
- 2 large cloves garlic, minced
- 1 teaspoon ground fennel
- ½ teaspoon dried red-pepper flakes
- ¾ cup dry white wine
- 1½ cups drained canned plum tomatoes
- 4 dozen littleneck clams, scrubbed
  Gremolata Crushed Potatoes, page 247
- 3 scallions, thinly sliced lengthwise

1. In a large saucepan of boiling water, cook the sausages for 5 minutes. Drain and let cool. Cut the sausages into ½-inch slices.

2. In a large pot, melt the butter over moderately low heat. Add the onions, sliced fennel, garlic, ground fennel, and red-pepper flakes. Cover and cook, stirring occasionally, until the vegetables are soft and lightly browned, about 20 minutes.

3. Increase the heat to high, add the wine, and bring just to a boil. Add the tomatoes and bring to a boil. Reduce the heat to moderate and simmer, stirring occasionally, until the sauce thickens slightly, about 15 minutes. Stir in the sausages.

4. Discard any clams that have broken shells or that do not clamp shut when tapped. Increase the heat to high and stir in the clams. Cover and cook just until the clams begin to open, about 3 minutes. Remove the open clams. Continue to cook, covered, removing the clams as they open. Discard any clams that do not open. Increase the heat to high and boil until the juices thicken slightly, about 5 minutes.

5. Place a scoop of the potatoes in the center of each of 6 large plates. Arrange the clams around the potatoes. Spoon the sausage and fennel mixture over the clams, garnish with the scallions, and serve.

—GEORGE GERMON AND JOHANNE KILLEEN, AL FORNO, PROVIDENCE, RHODE ISLAND

SPICY SHRIMP CAPRI

The Italian flavors of ripe tomatoes, brine-cured olives, and capers work beautifully with shrimp. Dried chile peppers add just the right amount of heat to the sauce. This quick and easy dish is also good served over pasta; linguine would be a good choice.

WINE RECOMMENDATION
High acidity and crispness are essential in any wine that accompanies this dish. Fortunately, almost all of the white wines of Northern and Central Italy share these characteristics. For example, try a lemony, unoaked sauvignon from Friuli.

SERVES 4

- ⅓ cup olive oil
- 3 cloves garlic
- 2 small dried red chile peppers, split and seeded
- 1 pound large shrimp, shelled and deveined
- 1 tablespoon capers, rinsed
- 12 brine-cured black olives, halved and pitted
- 12 cherry tomatoes, halved
- ½ cup dry white wine
- 1 tablespoon lemon juice
- 1 tablespoon chopped fresh parsley
- ½ teaspoon salt
- ⅛ teaspoon fresh-ground black pepper
- 3 tablespoons butter

1. In a large frying pan, heat the oil over moderately high heat. Add the garlic and chile peppers and cook, stirring frequently, until the garlic is golden and the peppers are dark brown. Discard the garlic and peppers.

2. Add the shrimp and cook, stirring, for 1 minute. Add the capers, olives, and tomatoes and cook until the tomatoes are softened but still hold their shape, about 1 minute.

3. Add the wine, lemon juice, parsley, salt, and black pepper. Boil for 1 minute. Add the butter, 1 tablespoon at a time, stirring gently until blended. Serve immediately.

—MARGARET AND G. FRANCO ROMAGNOLI

HALIBUT IN CAPERED BASIL MARINARA

A simple and flavorful sauce that is wonderful with halibut or any other firm-fleshed white fish, such as striped bass or whiting. Serve the remaining sauce over spaghetti to accompany the fish.

WINE RECOMMENDATION
The high acidity level and the piquancy of this dish demand a crisp white wine with some character. Vernaccia di San Gimignano from Tuscany should work nicely.

SERVES 4

    3   tablespoons olive oil
    1   onion, chopped
    1   28-ounce can crushed tomatoes
    1   tablespoon capers, rinsed
    1   teaspoon sugar
    ½   teaspoon salt
    ½   teaspoon fresh-ground black pepper
    ¼   cup (packed) shredded fresh basil
    4   halibut steaks (8 ounces each), about
        1 inch thick

1. Heat the oven to 350°. In a medium saucepan, heat the oil over moderate heat. Add the onion and cook, stirring frequently, until softened but not browned, about 5 minutes. Add the tomatoes, capers, sugar, salt, and pepper. Bring to a boil. Stir in the basil, reduce the heat to moderately low, and simmer until the sauce is reduced by one third, about 10 minutes.

2. Pour the sauce into a baking dish just large enough to hold the fish in a single layer. Add the fish steaks and baste with the sauce. Cover and bake until the fish is just opaque throughout, 15 minutes.

3. Transfer the fish to plates or a platter and spoon some of the sauce over it.

—CARL QUAGLIATA, GIOVANNI'S, CLEVELAND

SEAFOOD STEW WITH ROASTED RED PEPPER PESTO

The fresh flavors of the sea are highlighted in this easy-to-prepare stew that is garnished with garlicky croutons and red pepper pesto. Pureed roasted red pepper adds body and a touch of sweetness to the pesto sauce, which, like the classic version, is prepared with fresh basil and a little Parmesan cheese.

WINE RECOMMENDATION
The complex flavors of this dish require a white wine that can hold its own in busy company. A full-bodied white from Southern Italy, such as Mastroberardino's Greco di Tufo or D'Angelo's Vigna dei Pini, would work. A dry sparkling wine could also be quite delicious.

SERVES 4

1 14-ounce can tomatoes

¼ teaspoon fennel seeds

1 tablespoon olive oil

2 leeks, white and tender green parts only, finely chopped and washed well

1 onion, finely chopped

4 cloves garlic, 3 finely chopped, 1 left whole

3 cups Fish Stock, page 77, or 1½ cups bottled clam juice plus 1½ cups water

1 cup dry white wine

1½ teaspoons minced fresh thyme, or ½ teaspoon dried

1 bay leaf

Salt and fresh-ground black pepper

8 ¾-inch slices French bread

12 mussels, scrubbed and debearded

½ pound sea scallops

½ pound large shrimp, shelled and deveined

¼ cup Roasted Red Pepper Pesto, page 173

1. In a food processor, puree the tomatoes with their liquid. Grind the fennel seeds in a mortar or finely chop them with a large knife. Set aside.

2. In a large stainless-steel pot, heat the oil over moderate heat. Add the leeks, onion, and chopped garlic, cover, reduce the heat to low, and cook, stirring occasionally, until tender, about 10 minutes. Stir in the pureed tomatoes, the stock, wine, thyme, ground fennel, bay leaf, and ¼ teaspoon each salt and pepper and bring to a boil. Reduce the heat and simmer, stirring occasionally, for 20 minutes.

3. Meanwhile, heat the broiler. Toast the bread slices until golden and crisp. Let cool slightly, then rub each crouton on both sides with the whole garlic clove.

4. Discard any mussels that have broken shells or that don't clamp shut when

tapped. Add the mussels to the pot. Cover, increase the heat to moderate, and cook until they begin to open, about 3 minutes. Add the scallops and shrimp and simmer, stirring occasionally, until just done, about 3 minutes. Discard the bay leaf and season the stew with salt and pepper.

5. Ladle the stew into bowls. Top each serving with a dollop of the Roasted Red Pepper Pesto and serve with the croutons.

—GEORGIA CHAN DOWNARD

ROASTED RED PEPPER PESTO

You can substitute 1 whole roasted red pepper from a jar, rinsed and patted dry, for the freshly roasted one.

MAKES ABOUT ⅔ CUP

- 1 small red bell pepper
- ½ cup fresh basil leaves
- 1 small clove garlic, minced
- 2 teaspoons grated Parmesan cheese
- ½ tablespoon olive oil
- ½ teaspoon balsamic vinegar

1. Roast the pepper over an open flame or broil, turning with tongs until charred all over, about 10 minutes. When the pepper is cool enough to handle, pull off the skin. Remove the stem, seeds, and ribs.

2. In a food processor or blender, combine the roasted pepper, basil, garlic, Parmesan, oil, and vinegar and puree until almost smooth.

MAKE IT AHEAD

The pesto sauce can be prepared up to 4 hours ahead and kept covered at room temperature.

Adriatic Fish Stew with Clams, Calamari, and Shrimp

In the Marches region, on Italy's eastern coast, it is said that a traditional *brodetto* should be made with exactly thirteen different kinds of fish — and Adriatic fish at that. But here in the States we're not so fussy. Use fresh, firm-fleshed, nonoily fish, such as whiting, gray mullet, halibut, red snapper, sea bass, monkfish, and haddock, and you'll turn out a great, if nontraditional, brodetto. The skate, though, is essential, more for the texture that it imparts than the flavor. The addition of vinegar sets this recipe apart from other Italian fish stews.

WINE RECOMMENDATION
A good Verdicchio, from Italy's Adriatic coast, seems ideal for this dish. Slightly more flavorful than many other Italian white wines, and slightly oily in texture, it will contribute to the interplay of delicacy and intensity that the dish itself offers.

SERVES 6

- 12 ½-inch-thick slices Italian bread
- ½ cup plus 3 tablespoons olive oil
- 3 cloves garlic, halved lengthwise, 2 crushed
- ½ pound cleaned small calamari bodies, cut into ¼-inch rings, tentacles halved
- 1 large onion, thinly sliced
- 5 pounds assorted nonoily fish, cleaned, filleted, and cut into 3-inch pieces; heads, bones, and tails reserved and cut into 3-inch pieces
- ½ pound medium shrimp, shelled and deveined, shells reserved
- ½ cup dry white wine
- ½ cup water
- ½ cup white-wine vinegar
- 2 cups canned tomatoes with their liquid, coarsely chopped
  Salt and fresh-ground black pepper
- ½ pound cleaned skate wing
- 1 pound cherrystone clams, scrubbed
- 2 tablespoons minced flat-leaf parsley

1. Heat the oven to 350°. Put the bread on a baking sheet and brush with 3 tablespoons of the oil. Toast in the oven until lightly browned, about 20 minutes. Rub the croutons on one side with the halved garlic.

2. Bring a medium saucepan of water to a boil over moderately high heat. Add the calamari, stir once, and drain immediately. Rinse the calamari with cold water and drain thoroughly.

3. In a large, deep stainless-steel frying pan, heat the remaining ½ cup oil over moderate heat. Add the onion and crushed garlic and cook, stirring, until the onion is

translucent, about 7 minutes. Discard the garlic and transfer the onion to a bowl.

4. Add the fish heads, bones and tails and the shrimp shells to the pan, increase the heat to high, and cook, stirring, for 5 minutes. Add ¼ cup of the wine and cook, stirring, until slightly reduced, about 2 minutes. Stir in the water. Strain the mixture, pressing the bones firmly to get all the liquid. Wipe out the pan and return the liquid to it.

5. Add the onion to the pan with the remaining ¼ cup wine and the vinegar and bring to a boil over over moderate heat. Simmer until the liquid has reduced by half, about 3 minutes. Add the tomatoes with their juice and season with salt and pepper. Simmer for 5 minutes, crushing the tomatoes with a wooden spoon. Cover and cook for 5 minutes, stirring occasionally.

6. Spread the firmer fish (skate, monkfish, and halibut) in the pan in a single layer. Cook over moderate heat for 2 minutes, then turn the fish over. Add the more delicate fish (red snapper, sea bass, whiting, haddock, and gray mullet) and the shrimp to the pan. Discard any clams that have broken shells or that do not clamp shut when tapped, and add the clams to the pan. The sauce should barely cover the fish; if necessary, add a little water. Cover, reduce the heat to moderately low, and simmer until the fish is just done and most of the clams have opened, about 10 minutes.

7. Transfer the fish, shrimp, and opened clams to a large serving bowl and cover loosely with foil. Bring the broth to a boil over moderately high heat and boil until reduced to about 4 cups, removing the clams as they open. Stir in the calamari and heat briefly to rewarm it. Spoon the sauce and calamari over the seafood, sprinkle with the parsley, and serve with the croutons.

—G. FRANCO ROMAGNOLI

ROASTED HERB-STUFFED SNAPPER WITH EGGPLANT-TOMATO COMPOTE

With its complex flavor and texture, this Eggplant-Tomato Compote is delicious as a robust accompaniment for roasted whole snapper. Or serve it on its own over shredded lettuce or with chunks of bread.

WINE RECOMMENDATION

A wine delicate enough for the fish but intense enough for the compote? The dry, fruity white wine called Arneis, from the Piedmont region, is just that.

SERVES 4

Eggplant-Tomato Compote

½ cup extra-virgin olive oil

1 small onion minced

2 large cloves garlic, thinly sliced

1 large eggplant, cut into ¼-inch dice

1 pound plum tomatoes (about 5), peeled, seeded, and chopped, or one 28-ounce can tomatoes, drained and chopped

1 small zucchini, halved lengthwise, seeded, and cut into ½-inch dice

¼ cup chopped red bell pepper

¼ cup Niçoise olives, pitted and chopped

2 tablespoons minced fresh herbs, such as thyme, basil, oregano, and flat-leaf parsley

Salt and fresh-ground black pepper

¼ cup extra-virgin olive oil

1 teaspoon lime juice

⅛ teaspoon dried red-pepper flakes

14 large fresh basil leaves

4 red snappers (1¼ to 1½ pounds each), cleaned

4 sprigs fresh thyme

4 sprigs fresh oregano

4 sprigs fresh tarragon

4 sprigs flat-leaf parsley

1 teaspoon coarse salt

1. For the compote, in a large saucepan, heat the oil over moderate heat. Add the onion and cook, stirring frequently, until translucent, about 3 minutes. Add the garlic and cook for 1 minute. Stir in the eggplant, tomatoes, zucchini, and bell pepper. Bring to a simmer and cook, stirring occasionally, until most of the liquid has evaporated and the vegetables are soft, about 15 minutes.

2. Add the olives and herbs. Season with salt and pepper. Cook for 3 minutes to blend the flavors. Remove from the heat.

3. Meanwhile, in a small saucepan, warm the oil until barely hot to the touch. Add the lime juice, red-pepper flakes, and 6 of the basil leaves. Remove from the heat and let steep for 30 minutes. Strain the basil oil.

4. Heat the oven to 500°. Brush a large baking sheet or shallow roasting pan with some of the basil oil. Rinse the fish and dry with paper towels. Stuff each snapper with 1 sprig each of the thyme, oregano, tarragon, and parsley and 2 of the remaining basil leaves.

5. Arrange the fish on the baking sheet. Brush with the remaining basil oil and sprinkle with the salt. Roast until nicely browned and just opaque throughout, about 15 minutes. Serve with the compote.

—MARK MILITELLO, MARK'S PLACE, MIAMI

EGGPLANT

If there is an Italian vegetable that wins a prize for versatility, it is the *melanzana,* or eggplant. It is sautéed, baked, broiled, grilled, and steamed. In fact, the only way it is not eaten in Italy is raw. Eggplants come in a variety of shapes and sizes: there are round white or deep yellow ones, the baby purple eggplants, and the larger teardrop shape.

Cooks in Italy, as everywhere, disagree about whether or not an eggplant should be peeled. It seems to be a matter of personal preference. But keep in mind that an eggplant that is overripe or has been stored for a long time will have a tough skin that will not soften during cooking, so it generally is a good idea to peel it.

There also is disagreement about salting eggplants. Once done to rid them of their bitterness, modern farming methods have just about eliminated that as a factor. It is true, however, that eggplant that has been salted will absorb much less oil during frying than eggplant that has not been.

HOTEL PALUMBO'S BAKED STRIPED BASS

With the Adriatic and Mediterranean seas and freshwater lakes and streams, fresh fish is available year-round in Italy. Whole striped bass is a local favorite. Here it is stuffed with herbs, quickly panfried to crisp the skin, then baked.

WINE RECOMMENDATION

A wimpy white wine would taste simply boring with this simple, delicious dish. Turn instead to a rich white from Southern Italy, such as a Sicilian white or a characterful Fiano di Avellino.

SERVES 4

- 6 tablespoons olive oil
- 1 striped bass (about 3 pounds) or other firm-fleshed white fish, cleaned
- ½ teaspoon salt
- ¼ teaspoon fresh-ground black pepper
- 2 cloves garlic, crushed
- 2 sprigs fresh parsley
- 5 sprigs fresh mint
- 2 sprigs fresh oregano, or ½ teaspoon dried
- ¼ cup dry white wine

1. Heat the oven to 425°. In a large oven-proof frying pan, heat the oil over high heat until hot, about 3 minutes.

2. Meanwhile, rinse the fish and dry with paper towels. Rub the inside of the fish with the salt and pepper. Stuff with the garlic, parsley, mint, and oregano.

3. Add the fish to the pan and cook until the underside is browned, about 1 minute. Turn the fish and brown on the second side, about 1 minute. Remove from the heat.

4. Add the wine to the pan and tightly cover with aluminum foil. Bake until the fish is opaque and firm to the touch, about 15 minutes.

5. To serve, fillet the fish and spoon some of the cooking liquid over each serving.

—HOTEL PALUMBO, RAVELLO, ITALY

FENNEL-SCENTED GRILLED TROUT

To many Italians, grilling is the preferred way to cook fish. The result is nicely scented with smoke and crisp on the outside, with tender and moist flesh. Here, whole trout are grilled with sliced fennel for a quick and easy dish that's packed with flavor.

WINE RECOMMENDATION
The simple finesse of this dish would be lost with an oaky white wine. Choose a simple, unoaked Italian white wine such as Orvieto to achieve the best balance between the food and the wine.

SERVES 4

2 fennel bulbs (about 1 pound each), cut lengthwise into ¼-inch slices, feathery tops reserved

About 3 tablespoons extra-virgin olive oil

2 teaspoons coarse salt

4 trout (10 to 12 ounces each), cleaned

2 teaspoons Ricard or other anise-flavored aperitif

Lemon wedges, for garnish

1. Light the grill or heat the broiler. Brush the fennel lightly with oil and sprinkle with 1 teaspoon of the salt. Rinse the fish and dry with paper towels. Brush the trout inside and out with oil and sprinkle all over with the remaining 1 teaspoon salt. Drizzle ½ teaspoon of the Ricard into each cavity, then stuff each fish with the reserved fennel tops.

2. Grill or broil the trout and fennel for 4 minutes. Turn and cook until the fish is browned and just opaque throughout and the fennel is tender, about 4 minutes longer.

3. Transfer the fish and fennel to plates. Drizzle each fish with ½ teaspoon of the remaining oil and serve with the lemon wedges.

—GEORGE GERMON AND JOHANNE KILLEEN, AL FORNO, PROVIDENCE, RHODE ISLAND

GIAMBOTTA OF SQUASH AND KOHLRABI WITH TILEFISH

Instead of tilefish, you can try cod, salmon, or pompano, either fillets or whole small fish, or bigger fish cut into large pieces.

WINE RECOMMENDATION
The fairly intense flavor of this dish calls for a white wine that is more flavorful than is typical of most Italian whites. Try one from the South of Italy, such as Greco di Tufo, or a Sicilian white.

SERVES 4 TO 6

1 cup chopped fresh parsley

1½ pounds tilefish fillets or steaks

½ pound red potatoes, cut into 1-inch pieces

2 large strips lemon zest

½ cup extra-virgin olive oil

1 large piece smoked bacon rind (8 by 4 inches), or 2 small smoked ham hocks

2 large leeks (white and light-green parts only), cut crosswise into thin slices and washed well

1 small bulb celeriac, peeled and cut into ½-inch pieces

3 ribs celery, cut on the diagonal into ½-inch slices

4 small kohlrabi, peeled and cut into small wedges

6 cloves garlic, minced

3 to 4 sprigs fresh thyme, or 1 teaspoon dried
   Pinch dried red-pepper flakes

2 bay leaves

1½ teaspoons salt

1 pound yellow summer squash, cut into 1-inch pieces

½ small spaghetti squash, peeled, seeded, and cut into ½-inch cubes (optional)

1 cup water

2 tablespoons white-wine vinegar

1. Set aside ¼ cup of the parsley and the fish. In a large heavy pot, combine all of the remaining ingredients. Cover, bring to a simmer over moderately high heat, and cook, stirring occasionally, until the potatoes are tender, about 30 minutes. Discard the bay leaves and bacon rind.

2. Put the fish on top of the vegetables, cover, and cook until just opaque throughout, 5 to 7 minutes. Sprinkle with the remaining ¼ cup parsley and serve.

—ANNE DISRUDE

MAKE IT AHEAD

You can cook the vegetables several days ahead. Let cool completely, then cover and refrigerate. Reheat before adding and cooking the fish.

TUSCAN BEANS WITH TUNA, PANCETTA, AND LEMON

This is the most Tuscan of all dishes—it combines their love of beans with cooking in terra-cotta in a wood-fired brick oven. The beans can be eaten on their own as a vegetable or served over a slice of Tuscan bread that has been toasted and then rubbed with garlic.

WINE RECOMMENDATION This heartwarming dish needs a gutsy white wine, such as a good-quality pinot bianco, chardonnay, or pinot grigio from the Alto Adige region.

SERVES 8

- ¾ pound (about 2 cups) dried white beans, rinsed and picked over
- ¼ cup olive oil
- 12 large fresh sage leaves
- 4 large cloves garlic
- ¼ pound thinly sliced pancetta or prosciutto, cut into 1-inch pieces
- ½ teaspoon salt
- 2 tablespoons lemon juice
- 1 6½-ounce can tuna packed in olive oil, drained
- Fresh-ground black pepper

1. Soak the beans overnight in enough cold water to cover by at least 2 inches. Or, bring the beans to a boil, cover, remove from the heat, and let sit for 1 hour. Drain.

2. Heat the oven to 400°. In a medium casserole, combine the beans, oil, sage, garlic, pancetta, and salt. Cover tightly and bake, stirring occasionally, until the beans are tender, about 1½ hours.

3. Stir the lemon juice and tuna into the beans and bake, uncovered, 10 minutes longer. Season with pepper, and serve.

—GIULIANO BUGIALLI

MAKE IT AHEAD

The beans can be prepared through step 2 up to 2 days ahead. Cool completely and refrigerate. Reheat before adding the lemon juice and tuna.

PASTA FRITTATA

Frittatas, open-faced omelets, are one of the most versatile dishes in Italian cooking—they can be served hot or cold any time of the day, and the fillings are limited only by the cook's imagination. A well-seasoned oven-proof skillet, preferably cast iron, or oven-proof nonstick skillet is best for cooking frittatas. Any leftover pasta will work well in this recipe.

WINE RECOMMENDATION
Many people believe that eggs and wine don't go together, and the combination is certainly not one of the easiest. Sparkling wines go beautifully with eggs, though; an Italian classic-method bubbly or even a Champagne might amaze you with this dish.

SERVES 6

½ ounce dried porcini mushrooms

½ cup uncooked elbow macaroni, or 1¼ cups cooked pasta

2 teaspoons olive oil

2½ tablespoons butter

1 large onion, chopped

10 large eggs

4 large plum tomatoes, peeled, seeded, and chopped

2 tablespoons heavy cream

1 tablespoon chopped fresh marjoram, plus marjoram leaves, for garnish

1 teaspoon salt

1 teaspoon fresh-ground black pepper

¼ pound Gruyère cheese, grated (about 1¼ cups)

1. Put the porcini in a small bowl and pour boiling water to cover over them. Soak until softened, about 20 minutes. Remove the mushrooms and squeeze to remove as much liquid as possible. Coarsely chop.

2. Meanwhile, if using uncooked macaroni, in a medium saucepan of boiling, salted water, cook the macaroni until just done, about 8 minutes. Drain and toss with the oil. If using cooked pasta, toss with the oil.

3. Heat the oven to 400°. In a large oven-proof frying pan, melt 1½ tablespoons of the butter over moderate heat. Add the onion, reduce the heat to low, and cook, stirring occasionally, until golden and soft, about 12 minutes.

4. Meanwhile, in a large bowl, beat the eggs very lightly just to break the yolks. Stir in the tomatoes, porcini, cream, marjoram, salt, and pepper. Beat briefly to blend. Stir in the pasta.

5. Increase the heat under the frying pan to high and add the remaining 1 tablespoon butter. Heat until the butter is foam-

PIZZA AND BREADS

Asparagus and Parmesan Pan Pizza, page 199

BASIC PIZZA DOUGH

This recipe makes 1¾ pounds of dough, enough for seven 7-inch flat pizzas or two 9-inch deep-dish pizzas. The ingredients can be easily doubled if you wish to make a bigger batch.

MAKES 1¾ POUNDS

- 1 package dry yeast
- 1 tablespoon sugar
- 1½ cups lukewarm water (105° to 115°)
- 3 to 3¼ cups unbleached flour, preferably bread flour
- ½ teaspoon salt
- ¼ cup olive oil, preferably extra-virgin

1. In a small bowl, combine the yeast and sugar. Add the water and stir to mix. Set aside until it starts to bubble and foam, about 5 minutes.

2. Put 3 cups of flour in a large bowl. Stir in the salt, then make a well in the center of the flour. Pour the yeast mixture into the well and add the oil. Gradually stir in the flour, working toward the sides of the bowl. When all the flour is incorporated and the dough is still soft but beginning to mass together, turn out onto a lightly floured work surface.

3. Knead the dough, adding just enough additional flour until the dough is no longer sticky. (It is better that the dough be too soft than too stiff.) Continue to knead until the dough is smooth, shiny, and elastic, 10 to 15 minutes.

4. Shape the dough into a ball and place it in a large oiled bowl; turn the dough over to coat with the oil. Cover the bowl with plastic wrap. Put in a warm spot and let rise until doubled in bulk, 1 to 1½ hours.

5. Punch down the dough and reshape into a ball. Cover and refrigerate until doubled in bulk, 20 minutes to 1 hour.

6. Punch down the dough again. If making deep-dish pizza, divide the dough in half. If making flat pizza, divide the dough into 7 balls of equal weight (4 ounces).

—ANNE DISRUDE

MAKE IT AHEAD

The dough can be covered with plastic wrap and refrigerated for up to 1 day (let the dough come to room temperature before using), or wrapped well and frozen up to 2 months. Let thaw in the refrigerator.

Quick Semolina Pizza Dough

This dough takes almost no time at all to assemble, and it can be made ahead of time. You can refrigerate or freeze it, but it must be at room temperature before you cook it. This recipe uses baking powder rather than yeast, so there's no rising time.

MAKES ENOUGH FOR 4 INDIVIDUAL PIZZAS, 7 INCHES EACH

1 cup semolina flour*

⅓ cup hot water

1 teaspoon baking powder

½ teaspoon salt

1 tablespoon extra-virgin olive oil

1. In a food processor, combine the semolina flour, water, baking powder, salt, and oil. Process until the dough comes together, about 45 seconds.

2. Wrap the dough in plastic and let rest for at least 15 minutes, or up to 2 hours.

*Available at specialty food stores and Italian markets

—ANNE DISRUDE

MAKE IT AHEAD

The dough can be covered with plastic wrap and and refrigerated for up to a day (let the dough come to room temperature before using), or wrapped well and frozen for up to 1 month. Let thaw in the refrigerator.

FRESH TOMATO AND BASIL PIZZA

In Italy and throughout the world, pizza is associated with Naples, where the first *pizzeria* opened in 1830. The topping for these little pizzas reflects the straight-forward Neapolitan-style cuisine: olive oil, fresh tomatoes, and basil. Its simplicity makes it essential to use only the best ingredients.

WINE RECOMMENDATION
This pizza is simplicity itself, enabling you to go in many different directions with the wine, as long as you don't choose a full-bodied, tannic red. A dry Italian rosé would be lovely, as long as the wine is less than two years old; dry Lambrusco or an unoaked Italian white wine would work as well.

MAKES 4 INDIVIDUAL PIZZAS

1   pound (4 balls) Basic Pizza Dough, page 188

    Cornmeal, for sprinkling

¾   cup extra-virgin olive oil

2   medium tomatoes, cut into ¼-inch slices

½   teaspoon salt

⅛   teaspoon fresh-ground black pepper

¾   cup fresh basil leaves

1. Heat the oven and a pizza stone or baking tiles to 500° about 1 hour before baking. On a floured surface, roll out one ball of dough into a 7-inch round about ¼ inch thick. Sprinkle a baking sheet liberally with cornmeal and transfer the round of dough to the sheet. Repeat with the remaining dough.

2. Brush each round of dough with about 1½ tablespoons of the oil. Arrange the tomato slices on top and sprinkle with the salt and pepper. Scatter some basil leaves on top. Drizzle the remaining oil over all.

3. Carefully slide the pizzas onto the hot pizza stone or tiles. Bake until the bottom of the crust is browned, 8 to 10 minutes.

—ANNE DISRUDE

CRISP CRUSTS

Pizza stones and baking tiles are the home baker's ticket to a superior crust. These porous unglazed surfaces draw moisture from the bottom of the crust, leaving it wonderfully chewy and crisp.

Baking tiles (unglazed quarry tiles) are available from home improvement centers or tile shops. Purchase enough to cover an oven rack, allowing about 2 inches of space around the edges for air circulation.

The pizza stone or baking tiles should be placed on the bottom oven rack, closest to the heat source, and allowed to heat up for about 1 hour before baking.

OLIVE AND ROASTED RED PEPPER PIZZA

This is for people who like their pizza packed with flavor. Instead of a red sauce, a puree of anchovies, garlic, olive oil, and black olives is spread over the crust and topped with mozzarella and roasted red peppers. Serve these with a plate of marinated vegetables, such as artichoke hearts and mushrooms.

WINE RECOMMENDATION
This dish is flavorful enough that you could pour either a red wine or a white, but the presence of anchovies tips the scales toward white. To match the savory, vegetal, and slightly sweet flavors of the pizza topping, try a full-bodied white such as Fiano di Avellino, or even a new-style oaked Italian white.

MAKES 3 INDIVIDUAL PIZZAS

- 3 anchovy fillets, rinsed and patted dry
- 1 large clove garlic, crushed
- ¼ teaspoon fresh-ground black pepper
- ¼ cup olive oil
- 1 cup Kalamata or other brine-cured black olives, pitted
- ¾ pound (3 balls) Basic Pizza Dough, page 188
- Cornmeal, for sprinkling
- ¼ pound mozzarella, cut into 9 thin slices
- 1 red bell pepper, roasted, peeled, seeded, and finely chopped

1. Heat the oven and a pizza stone or baking tiles to 500° about 1 hour before baking. Put the anchovies, garlic, black pepper, and 2 tablespoons of the oil in a food processor and puree until almost liquefied. Add the olives and process until chopped but not pureed.

2. On a floured surface, roll out one ball of dough to a 7-inch round, about ¼ inch thick. Sprinkle a baking sheet liberally with cornmeal and transfer the round of dough to the sheet. Repeat with the remaining dough.

3. Brush each round of dough with about 1 teaspoon of the oil. Spread about ⅓ cup of the olive mixture evenly on each round. Drizzle with the remaining oil.

4. Carefully slide the pizzas onto the hot pizza stone or tiles. Bake until the bottom of the crust is lightly browned, 6 to 8 minutes. Remove from the oven, and place 3 slices of mozzarella on each crust. Sprinkle with the bell pepper, return to the oven, and bake until the cheese is melted, about 5 minutes.

—ANNE DISRUDE

ZUCCHINI AND SUN-DRIED TOMATO PAN PIZZA

Make sure you cook the zucchini in a large pan, without crowding, for the best texture and flavor. When tomatoes are in season, substitute one large fresh beefsteak tomato for the sun-dried tomatoes.

WINE RECOMMENDATION
This dish strikes its own lovely balance of flavors: sweet mozzarella versus earthy zucchini. Go for a light-bodied or medium-bodied red wine that's low in tannin, such as an inexpensive sangiovese from Tuscany.

MAKES 2 INDIVIDUAL PIZZAS

- 3 small zucchini, cut into ⅜-inch pieces
  Salt
- 1 tablespoon oil from sun-dried tomatoes
- 4 sun-dried tomatoes packed in oil, minced
- 3 cloves garlic, crushed
  Pinch dried red-pepper flakes
- 2 tablespoons minced fresh basil
  Fresh-ground black pepper
- ½ recipe Quick Semolina Pizza Dough, page 189
- ¼ pound mozzarella, diced (about ⅔ cup)

1. Put the zucchini in a colander and sprinkle with ½ teaspoon salt; toss and drain. Gently blot with a paper towel.

2. Meanwhile, in a large heavy frying pan, heat the oil over moderate heat. Add the sun-dried tomatoes, garlic, and red-pepper flakes. Cook, stirring frequently, until the garlic begins to soften, about 2 minutes. Increase the heat to high, add the zucchini, and toss. Cook, tossing frequently, until the zucchini is evenly browned, about 3 minutes. Remove from the heat and discard the garlic. Stir in the basil and season with salt and black pepper.

3. On a lightly floured surface, roll the dough into a log 1½ inches in diameter. Cut in half. Roll out each piece of dough into a 7-inch round about 1⁄16 inch thick. Cover with plastic wrap.

4. Heat a 9- or 10-inch cast-iron frying pan over moderately high heat. Put one of the dough rounds into the pan, reduce the heat to low, cover, and cook until the crust is dark brown on the bottom, about 3 minutes. (Check after 2 minutes and adjust the heat if necessary to avoid burning.)

5. Remove the crust from the pan. Scatter half the mozzarella over the crust and top with about ½ cup of the zucchini. Return the pizza to the pan and cook, covered, until the cheese melts, about 2 minutes. Repeat with the remaining dough, mozzarella, and zucchini.

—ANNE DISRUDE

ARTICHOKE AND GARLIC PAN PIZZA

These individual pizzas are made on the stove top in a cast-iron skillet. When you select artichokes, choose the biggest ones you can find, because they have the most flavorful hearts. This may seem like a lot of garlic, but simmering it with the artichokes mellows and sweetens it.

WINE RECOMMENDATION
Because artichokes sweeten whatever you consume with them, they can be very problematic for wine. One type of wine that does seem to work is brut (dry) sparkling wines. Italy's brut sparkling wines are ideal, because they tend to drier than French, Spanish, or American bubblies.

MAKES 4 INDIVIDUAL PIZZAS

4   large artichokes

½   lemon

2   heads garlic, cloves separated and peeled (about 24)

8   sprigs flat-leaf parsley

¼   cup extra-virgin olive oil

1½ teaspoons fresh thyme leaves

    Salt and fresh-ground black pepper

½   pound mozzarella, diced (about 1⅓ cups)

    Quick Semolina Pizza Dough, page 189

1. With a small sharp knife, cut the leaves from each artichoke, using a circular motion, until you reach the tender inner leaves. Cut the tops off the leaves and trim the artichoke heart down to the base, removing all the tough, fibrous outer skin. Cut each heart in half and cut out the choke. Rub the hearts all over with the lemon.

2. In a large bowl, combine the artichoke hearts, garlic, parsley, oil, thyme, ¼ teaspoon salt, and ¼ teaspoon pepper; toss to mix.

3. In a large stainless-steel saucepan, arrange the artichokes, with the garlic-parsley mixture, bottom-side down, and sprinkle with 3 tablespoons water. Cover tightly and cook over low heat, turning occasionally, until the artichokes are lightly browned and very tender, about 30 minutes. Add a few tablespoons of water after 10 minutes to prevent burning.

4. Remove the pan from the heat. Finely chop the garlic and parsley. In a small bowl, combine the mozzarella, garlic, and parsley. Slice the artichokes ¼ inch thick.

5. On a lightly floured surface, roll the dough into a log 1½ inches in diameter. Cut into four equal pieces. Roll out each piece of dough into a 7-inch round about 1/16 inch thick. Cover the rounds with plastic wrap.

6. Heat a 9- or 10-inch cast-iron frying pan over moderately high heat. Put one of the dough rounds into the pan, reduce the heat to low, cover, and cook until the crust is dark brown on the bottom, about 3 min-

194

utes. (Check after 2 minutes and adjust the heat if necessary to avoid burning.)

7. Remove the crust from the pan. Layer ⅓ cup of the mozzarella mixture and one quarter of the artichoke slices on the crust; season with salt and pepper. Brush the top with any remaining oil from the pan. Return the pizza to the pan and cook, covered, until the cheese melts, about 2 minutes. Repeat with the remaining dough, mozzarella mixture, and artichokes.

—ANNE DISRUDE

PIZZA TIPS

• Make the pizza dough well ahead of time. If you are using the Quick Semolina Pizza Dough, page 189, you can store it in the refrigerator or freezer. If you are using a yeast-risen dough, such as Basic Pizza Dough, page 188, it can be stored for an hour or so in the refrigerator, but for longer storage it should be frozen.

• Let frozen pizza dough thaw, then roll out, cover with plastic wrap, and let come to room temperature before topping and baking.

• Keep in mind that any vegetables you use should be thinly sliced or cut into small pieces so they will not be heavy or wet, which makes for a soggy or dense crust.

• Keep on hand some store-bought toppings, such as pesto, brine-cured olives, capers, roasted red peppers, artichoke hearts, and sun-dried tomatoes.

SCALLION AND OLIVE PAN PIZZA

Pungent, tender scallions braised with bay leaves and rosemary are offset by Gaeta olives and fresh goat cheese. Experiment with other varieties of onions such as red, sweet white, or Vidalia, when they are in season.

WINE RECOMMENDATION
Wines based on the sauvignon blanc grape are delicious with goat cheese. Besides complementing the goat cheese, a sauvignon from Northeastern Italy will provide a lean, crisp counterbalance to the flavorful olives.

MAKES 4 INDIVIDUAL PIZZAS

¼ cup extra-virgin olive oil

12 bunches scallions (white and light-green parts), cut into ½-inch slices, plus ¼ cup minced green tops

3 bay leaves

2 sprigs fresh rosemary plus 1 teaspoon minced

3 tablespoons water

¼ cup coarsely chopped olives, preferably Gaeta or Niçoise

¾ teaspoon salt

¼ teaspoon fresh-ground black pepper
   Quick Semolina Pizza Dough, page 189

¼ pound mild goat cheese, such as Montrachet, at room temperature

1. In a large heavy saucepan, heat the oil. Add the sliced scallions, bay leaves, rosemary sprigs, and water. Cover and cook over moderately low heat, stirring occasionally, until the scallions are very tender, about 20 minutes. Remove from the heat.

Discard the bay leaves and the rosemary sprigs. Stir in the olives, minced rosemary, salt, and pepper.

2. On a lightly floured surface, roll the dough into a log 1½ inches in diameter. Cut into 4 equal pieces. Roll out each piece into a 7-inch round. Cover with plastic wrap.

3. Heat a 9- or 10-inch cast-iron frying pan over moderately high heat. Put one of the dough rounds into the pan, reduce the heat to low, cover, and cook until the crust is dark brown on the bottom, about 3 minutes. (Check after 2 minutes and adjust the heat if necessary to avoid burning.)

4. Remove the crust from the pan. Spread with about 2 tablespoons of the goat cheese and top with about ½ cup of the cooked scallion mixture. Return the pizza to the pan and cook, covered, until the cheese melts, about 2 minutes. Sprinkle with 1 tablespoon of the minced scallion greens. Repeat with the remaining dough, goat cheese, and scallions.

—ANNE DISRUDE

Opposite: Artichoke and Garlic Pan Pizza (left), page 194, and Scallion and Olive Pan Pizza

ASPARAGUS AND PARMESAN PAN PIZZA

This topping is borrowed from Parma, where Parmigiano-Reggiano is made. Traditionally, asparagus is served simply with a blanket of Parmesan cheese. Here the asparagus is cut into pieces and cooked until tender, combined with onion and butter, and covered with shavings of the cheese to make an unusual pizza.

WINE RECOMMENDATION
Celebrate the vegetal flavors of this dish with a wine that lets them sing through. Vernaccia di San Gimignano, a medium-bodied white, will do just that.

MAKES 4 INDIVIDUAL PIZZAS

- 1½   pounds asparagus
- 3   tablespoons butter
- ½   cup diced red onion
- ¼   teaspoon salt
- ¼   teaspoon fresh-ground black pepper
  Quick Semolina Pizza Dough, page 189
- ½   pound mozzarella, diced (about 1⅓ cups)
  Small chunk Parmesan cheese, for shaving

1. Snap the tough ends off the asparagus and discard them. Cut the spears into 1-inch lengths if skinny, ½-inch pieces if fat. Reserve the tips. In a large pot of boiling salted water, cook the spears until almost tender, about 2 minutes. Add the tips and cook until tender, 2 minutes longer. Drain and pat dry with paper towels.

2. In a large frying pan, melt the butter over moderately low heat. Add the red onion and cook, stirring frequently, until softened, about 5 minutes. Stir in the asparagus and cook, tossing frequently, for about 2 minutes. Remove from the heat and season with the salt and pepper.

3. On a lightly floured surface, roll the dough into a log 1½ inches in diameter. Cut into four equal pieces. Roll out each piece of dough into a 7-inch round about ⅟₁₆ inch thick. Cover the rounds with plastic wrap.

4. Heat a 9- or 10-inch cast-iron frying pan over moderately high heat. Put one of the dough rounds into the pan and reduce the heat to low. Cover and cook until the crust is dark brown on the bottom, about 3 minutes. (Check after 2 minutes and reduce the heat if necessary to avoid burning.)

5. Remove the crust from the pan. Scatter about ⅓ cup of the mozzarella over the crust and top with about ¾ cup of the asparagus. Return the pizza to the pan and cook, covered, until the cheese melts, about 2 minutes. Using a vegetable peeler, cut shavings of the Parmesan onto the pizza. Repeat with the remaining dough, cheese, and asparagus.

—ANNE DISRUDE

EGGPLANT AND GOAT CHEESE DEEP-DISH PIZZA

Thick deep-dish pizza was developed in Chicago, where it has become a regional specialty. You will need a special pizza pan for this recipe with sides about 2 inches high. The pan should be wiped clean, not washed, so it will season.

WINE RECOMMENDATION
Despite the popular perception that red wine and cheese are made for each other, goat cheese and red wine don't get along too well. Try an earthy white wine that will echo the earthy flavor of the eggplant, such as a Tuscan chardonnay.

MAKES ONE 9-INCH PIZZA

- 3 small eggplant (about 2½ pounds)
- ⅓ cup coarse salt
- ½ cup olive oil
- ½ teaspoon minced fresh rosemary, or ¼ teaspoon dried
  Salt and fresh-ground black pepper
- 14 ounces (½ recipe) Basic Pizza Dough, page 188
- 5 to 6 ounces mild goat cheese, such as Montrachet

1. Cut 1 eggplant lengthwise into ¼-inch slices and trim to 4½ inches long. Peel the remaining 2 eggplants and cut into ½-inch cubes.

2. Sprinkle both sides of the eggplant slices with half of the salt and place on a rack to drain. Toss the cubed eggplant with the remaining coarse salt and place in a large colander to drain. Let stand for about 30 minutes.

3. Rinse the eggplant slices and cubes; drain well and pat dry between towels. Wrap in kitchen towels, place in a colander or on a rack, and weigh down, to force out more liquid. Let stand for 1 hour.

4. Heat the oven to 450°. Heat a large heavy frying pan over high heat. In batches, lightly brush the eggplant slices with oil, place in the pan, and cook until lightly browned, about 2 minutes on each side. Remove to a plate.

5. Add ¼ cup of oil to the pan and heat until almost smoking. Add the eggplant cubes and toss. Add the rosemary and cook, tossing occasionally, until the eggplant is browned around the edges, about 10 minutes. Season with salt and pepper.

6. To assemble the pizza, oil a 9-inch deep-dish pizza pan. Roll the dough out and fit it into the pan following the instructions in Shaping a Deep-Dish Pizza, page 201. Brush the dough with about 1 tablespoon of oil. Crumble the goat cheese over the dough. Cover with the cubed eggplant.

Arrange the eggplant slices in an overlapping pinwheel pattern on top. Drizzle with any remaining oil and sprinkle lightly with salt and pepper.

7. Bake in the middle of the oven until the crust is golden, about 20 minutes. Remove the pizza from the pan and let stand on a rack for 10 minutes before slicing, to allow the filling to set.

—ANNE DISRUDE

SHAPING A DEEP-DISH PIZZA

Roll out a 14-ounce ball of dough to a round that will comfortably line a 9-inch deep-dish pizza pan with an additional 1 inch for overlap.

Coat the pizza pan with a heavy film of olive oil to ensure a crisp crust. Drape the dough loosely over the pan and ease it into the bottom and up the sides of the pan.

After brushing the dough liberally with oil, top with the filling. Add the cheese first (if there is any) and any sauce last.

Using a pizza cutter or a small knife, trim off the dough about halfway up the sides of the pan, just above the top of the filling (the dough will rise as it bakes to contain all of the filling).

CALZONE DOUGH

The dough for calzones (savory Italian turnovers) is very similar to pizza dough, and in fact most recipes are interchangeable. This dough takes almost no time at all to assemble, and it can be made ahead of time.

MAKES ENOUGH FOR 4 CALZONE

1 package dry yeast

1 cup lukewarm water (105° to 115°)

¼ cup olive oil, preferably extra-virgin

2½ to 3 cups flour

1½ teaspoons salt

1. In a small bowl, sprinkle the yeast over the warm water. Set aside until it starts to bubble and foam, about 5 minutes. Stir in the oil.

2. *By hand*: In a large bowl, combine 2½ cups flour and the salt. Add the yeast mixture and stir until well blended. Turn out onto a lightly floured surface. Knead until smooth and elastic, 8 to 10 minutes, adding more flour if needed; the dough should remain slightly soft.

Food processor method: Combine the flour and salt in a food processor. With the machine running, add the yeast mixture and process until the dough is smooth and comes away from the sides of the bowl. Turn the dough out onto a lightly floured surface and knead briefly, adding more flour if needed.

Heavy-duty mixer method: In the large bowl of an electric mixer fitted with a dough hook, combine the flour and salt. With the mixer on low speed, gradually add the yeast mixture. Knead until the dough masses on the hook and becomes smooth and elastic, adding more flour as needed.

3. Put the dough in a lightly oiled bowl; turn to coat. Cover the bowl with plastic wrap. Put in a warm spot and let rise until doubled in volume, about 1 hour.

4. Punch down the dough and divide into 4 equal pieces.

—MICHELE SCICOLONE

MAKE IT AHEAD

The dough can be covered with plastic wrap and refrigerated for up to a day (let the dough return to room temperature before using), or wrapped well and frozen up to 1 month. Let thaw in the refrigerator.

CALZONE CON SALSICCIA

Calzones, just like pizza, originated in Naples and are simple, rustic fare. After you have experimented with this classic sausage and pepper filling, create one of your own with ingredients such as grilled or roasted vegetables and Fontina or ricotta salata cheese.

WINE RECOMMENDATION
This simple country dish begs for an equally rustic, unpretentious red wine that you can quaff without contemplation. A Montepulciano d'Abruzzo—inexpensive, delicious, and easy to drink—would be ideal.

MAKES 4 CALZONI

- 4 sweet or hot Italian sausages (about ¼ pound)
- 3 tablespoons olive oil, preferably extra-virgin
- 4 medium bell peppers, thinly sliced
- 3 medium onions, thinly sliced
- ½ to 1 teaspoon salt (depending on the saltiness of the sausage)
- ⅛ teaspoon fresh-ground black pepper
  Calzone Dough, page 202

1. Prick the sausages all over with a fork. Put into a medium frying pan with ½ inch of water, cover, and simmer over moderate heat until the water evaporates, about 20 minutes. Uncover and cook, turning occasionally, until the sausages are browned. Let cool. Cut into ¼-inch slices.

2. In a large frying pan, heat the olive oil over moderate heat. Add the bell peppers and cook, stirring frequently, for 5 minutes. Add the onions, salt, and black pepper. Cook until the peppers are soft and the onions are lightly browned, 15 to 20 minutes. Remove from the heat and let cool.

3. On a lightly floured surface, roll out each ball of dough to a 10-inch round. (If you have time, cover the dough with kitchen towels and plastic wrap and let it rest for 30 minutes; it will yield a more tender crust.)

4. Heat the oven to 450°. Grease a large baking sheet. Arrange the dough circles on the prepared sheet, with half of each circle off the edge of the sheet. Arrange the sausage slices over the half of each dough circle that is on the sheet, leaving a 1-inch border around the edge. Top with the peppers and onions. Fold the dough over the filling to form a half-moon. Press the edges together to seal. Crimp decoratively by folding the lower edge up and over the top edge at about ¾-inch intervals.

5. Bake on the lowest rack of the oven until brown and puffed, 20 to 25 minutes. Remove to a rack and let rest for 10 minutes before serving.

—MICHELE SCICOLONE

CALZONE MARGHERITA

The filling for this calzone is named after Italy's Queen Margherita, who apparently loved it because it bore her country's colors, with its red tomatoes, white cheese, and green basil. Use only ripe, meaty tomatoes for this filling (in winter, plum tomatoes are the best choice), and fresh mozzarella or imported buffalo mozzarella.

WINE RECOMMENDATION

A low-tannin, fresh-tasting young red wine would complement the simple, direct flavors of this food. Either an unoaked barbera (generally barbera wines that sell for under $15 are unoaked) or a Chianti that's less than three years old would be a good choice.

MAKES 4 CALZONI

1 pound tomatoes, peeled, seeded, and finely diced

½ teaspoon salt

½ pound fresh mozzarella, finely diced

¼ cup grated Parmesan cheese

2 tablespoons olive oil, preferably extra-virgin

2 medium cloves garlic, finely chopped

8 fresh basil leaves, minced, or ½ teaspoon dried

½ teaspoon dried oregano

⅛ teaspoon fresh-ground black pepper
   Calzone Dough, page 202

1. Put the tomatoes in a colander, sprinkle with the salt, and let drain for 30 minutes.

2. In a medium bowl, combine the mozzarella and Parmesan cheeses, the oil, garlic, basil, oregano, and pepper. Add the tomatoes and toss to mix.

3. On a lightly floured surface, roll out each ball of dough to a 10-inch circle. (If you have time, cover the dough with kitchen towels and plastic wrap, and let it rest for 30 minutes; it will yield a more tender crust.)

4. Heat the oven to 450°. Grease a large baking sheet. Arrange the dough circles on the sheet with half of each circle off the edge of the sheet. Put about ½ cup filling on the half of each circle that is on the sheet, leaving a 1-inch border around the edge. Fold the dough over the filling to form a half-moon. Press the edges together to seal. Crimp decoratively by folding the lower edge up and over the top edge at about ¾-inch intervals.

5. Bake on the lowest rack of the oven until brown and puffed, 20 to 25 minutes. Transfer to a rack and let rest for 10 minutes before serving.

—MICHELE SCICOLONE

ROSEMARY FOCACCIA

The main difference between focaccia and pizza is in the thickness of the dough—focaccia is substantially thicker. Some toppings are elaborate, but many are simple, such as this sprinkling of sea salt, olive oil, and fresh herbs. "Dimpling" the dough before it is baked traps little pools of oil. Focaccia makes a wonderful snack, accompaniment to soup or salad, or hors d'oeuvre.

MAKES ONE 10-INCH ROUND FOCACCIA

- ½ cup sliced shallots (about 8 medium)
- 3 to 4 small sprigs fresh rosemary, or ½ teaspoon dried
- ½ teaspoon coarse salt
- ½ teaspoon fresh-ground black pepper
- 5 tablespoons extra-virgin olive oil
- 1 pound Basic Pizza Dough, page 188

1. Heat the oven to 425°. In a small bowl, toss the shallots, rosemary, salt, and pepper with 3½ tablespoons of the oil.

2. On a lightly floured surface, roll out the dough to a 10-inch circle about ½ inch thick.

3. Heat a heavy 12-inch oven-proof frying pan over high heat for 1 minute. Add the remaining 1½ tablespoons oil. When the oil is shimmering, remove from the heat and carefully lay the rolled-out dough in the pan.

4. Using your fingertips, make indentations all over the dough. Spread the shallot mixture on top. Bake the focaccia in the upper third of the oven until browned on top, about 25 minutes. Remove to a wire rack to cool for 15 minutes before cutting into wedges.

—ANNE DISRUDE

205

HERBED SKILLET FLATBREAD

This savory flatbread is scented with rosemary and garlic and fills the air with a wonderful aroma while it bakes. It can be served as a snack or instead of other bread with a meal. One of the baked loaves can be cooled, wrapped in foil, and frozen to enjoy later.

MAKES 2 ROUND FLAT LOAVES

- 1 tablespoon sugar
- 1½ cups lukewarm water (105° to 115°)
- 1 package dry yeast
- 3¼ to 3¾ cups bread flour
- 1 teaspoon chopped fresh rosemary, or ½ teaspoon dried, plus 4 sprigs fresh rosemary, for garnish (optional)
- 1 tablespoon coarse salt
- 1 teaspoon coarse-ground black pepper
- ½ cup olive oil, preferably extra-virgin
- 4 cloves garlic, thinly sliced

1. In a medium bowl, dissolve the sugar in ½ cup of the water. Sprinkle the yeast on top and set aside until it starts to foam, about 5 minutes.

2. In a large bowl, combine 3¼ cups of the flour, the chopped rosemary, 2 teaspoons of the salt, and ½ teaspoon of the pepper.

3. Stir ¼ cup of the oil and the remaining 1 cup water into the yeast mixture. Make a well in the center of the flour and add the liquid ingredients. Stir until well mixed.

4. Turn the dough out onto a floured surface and knead until smooth and elastic, about 15 minutes. Use only as much additional flour as necessary to prevent sticking and to form a slightly soft dough.

5. Form the dough into a ball and put into a large oiled bowl. Turn to coat with oil. Cover the bowl with plastic wrap and a towel. Put in a warm spot and let the dough rise until doubled in bulk, about 1 hour. Punch down the dough and let rise until doubled in bulk again, about 1 hour.

6. Heat the oven to 400°. Place a 12- to 14-inch cast-iron frying pan in the oven to heat.

7. Divide the dough in half. Return half the dough to the bowl, cover, and refrigerate while you make the first loaf. (If you'd prefer to make only one loaf, the other half of the dough can be frozen and baked at a later time.) On a lightly floured surface, roll the dough out to a ½-inch-thick round. With a sharp knife, score lightly in a crisscross pattern.

8. Remove the pan from the oven and coat the bottom and sides with 1 tablespoon of the oil. Put the dough in the pan. Press the edges down to even the thickness. Scatter half of the garlic over the dough

ROSEMARY GRISSINI

Grissini (breadsticks), as well as bread, are usually served with an Italian meal. But they also make delicious appetizers, especially with a slice of prosciutto wrapped around one end. Kept in an airtight container, the breadsticks will remain fresh for several days.

MAKES 3 DOZEN BREADSTICKS

- 3 packages dry yeast
- 1 cup lukewarm water (105° to 115°)
- 1 cup bread flour
- 1½ cups whole wheat flour
- ¾ cup coarse semolina
- 1 teaspoon salt
- 2 tablespoons plus 1 teaspoon extra-virgin olive oil
- 2 tablespoons finely chopped fresh rosemary, or 2 teaspoons dried

1. In a small bowl, dissolve the yeast in the water. Set aside until it starts to foam, about 10 minutes.

2. On a work surface, combine the flours, ½ cup of the semolina, and the salt. Shape the dry ingredients into a mound, make a well in the center, and add 2 tablespoons of the oil. Pour the dissolved yeast into the well, a little at a time, mixing with a fork in a circular motion, and drawing in the flours until all the ingredients are combined and a dough forms. Add the rosemary to the dough and knead until it is smooth and elastic, about 10 minutes.

3. Coat the inside of a large bowl with the remaining 1 teaspoon oil. Form the dough into a ball and put it in the oiled bowl, turning to coat all sides with oil. Cover the bowl with a cloth. Put in a warm spot and let rise until at least doubled in bulk, about 2 hours.

4. Heat the oven to 350°. Sprinkle a work surface with 2 to 3 tablespoons of the semolina. Punch down the dough. Roll the dough out to a rectangle approximately 8 by 9 inches and ½ inch thick. Cut crosswise into ¼-inch strips and roll gently into sticks about 10 inches long.

5. Sprinkle a heavy baking sheet with the remaining semolina and arrange the breadsticks about 1 inch apart on the baking sheet. Cover with a towel and let rise in a warm place for 10 minutes.

6. Bake in the middle of the oven for about 30 minutes, until lightly golden and crisp. Transfer to a rack to cool slightly. Serve warm.

—LORENZA DE'MEDICI

GRILLED FONTINA AND GREEN OLIVE SANDWICHES

Although these are best when made with Italian Fontina cheese, any good melting cheese such as Port-Salut, Muenster, or Monterey Jack will work well.

WINE RECOMMENDATION
Here you need a white wine flavorful enough to stand up to the assertive taste of the olives. A better Orvieto, such as Antinori's, or an Italian sauvignon would be appropriate.

MAKES 4 SANDWICHES

8   thin slices firm white or whole wheat bread, crusts removed

8   teaspoons mayonnaise

¼   pound Fontina or other melting cheese, coarsely shredded (about 1 cup)

8 to 10 brine-cured green olives, pitted and chopped

8   teaspoons butter

1. Spread each slice of bread with 1 teaspoon of mayonnaise. Top 4 slices of the bread with the cheese. Mound the olives in the center over the cheese and top with the remaining bread, mayonnaise-side down.

2. In a heavy medium frying pan, melt 2 teaspoons of the butter over moderately low heat. Put two sandwiches in the pan and cook until light golden brown on the bottom, 2 to 3 minutes. Add 2 more teaspoons of butter to the pan, turn the sandwiches with a spatula, and cook until golden brown on the second side, 2 to 3 minutes. Transfer to a platter. Repeat with the remaining butter and sandwiches. Serve hot.

—JIM FOBEL

FONTINA

Although Italian law specifies that Fontina cheese (more properly called Fontina d'Aosta) can only be made in the Val d'Aosta region of Northern Italy, this buttery cheese with a nutty flavor is widely copied outside of Italy. The French version, known as Fontal, is softer, sweeter, and more buttery, while Danish Fontina is tart and Swedish Fontina has a fuller yet less complex flavor.

One easy way to spot the Italian original, considered by many to be the best of the bunch, is by the rind, which ranges in color from light to dark brown; the others sport red rinds. Fontina d'Aosta is traditionally used to make *fonduta*, a fondue topped with white truffles.

SIDE DISHES

Baked Fennel with Parmesan, page 234

ARTICHOKE AND POTATO STEW WITH MINT

Chopped fresh mint combined with garlic and olive oil makes an aromatic and savory broth for artichoke hearts and potatoes. Serve the stew with garlic-rubbed grilled bread for sopping up the juices.

SERVES 4

4 artichokes

½ lemon

¼ cup extra-virgin olive oil, plus more for drizzling

3 large cloves garlic, 2 finely chopped, 1 halved

3 new potatoes (about ½ pound), peeled, cut into eighths, and rinsed

3 tablespoons chopped flat-leaf parsley

¼ cup chopped fresh mint

Salt and fresh-ground black pepper

1 cup water

4 thick slices country bread

Grated Pecorino Romano cheese (optional), for serving

1. Working with one artichoke at a time, break off and discard the tough outer leaves until you reach the tender pale-yellow leaves. Cut off the top half of the leaves. Using a small sharp knife, trim off the tough, dark-green areas from the artichoke bottom and stem. Rub the lemon half over the cut surfaces of the artichoke to prevent darkening. Trim the stems to 1 inch. Quarter the artichoke and cut away the hairy choke. Cut each quarter lengthwise in half.

2. In a medium stainless-steel saucepan, heat the oil over moderately low heat. Add the chopped garlic and cook, stirring frequently, until fragrant, about 2 minutes. Add the artichokes, potatoes, parsley, and mint and season with salt and pepper. Cook, stirring, until heated through, 2 to 3 minutes. Add the water, cover, reduce the heat to moderate, and cook, stirring occasionally, until the vegetables are tender, about 20 minutes.

3. Just before serving, grill or toast the bread. Rub with the halved garlic clove and drizzle lightly with oil.

4. Ladle the stew into shallow soup bowls. Grind pepper over the top and sprinkle with a few drops of oil. If desired, sprinkle lightly with cheese. Serve with the garlic toast.

—VIANA LA PLACE

BROCCOLI WITH GARLIC CHIPS

In Italy, vegetables are often cooked in boiling water until almost tender, then sautéed in olive oil. That is the technique used for this very simple broccoli dish. Crisp, golden garlic slices add lots of flavor and make an attractive garnish.

SERVES 4

1¼ pounds broccoli

¼ cup extra-virgin olive oil

6 cloves garlic, thinly sliced lengthwise

Salt and fresh-ground black pepper

1. Peel the broccoli stalks. Cut each stalk lengthwise to make long skinny stalks about ½ inch thick.

2. In a large frying pan, bring 1 cup of water to a boil over high heat. Add the broccoli and cook, uncovered, turning once, until tender and most of the water has evaporated, 5 to 6 minutes. Transfer the broccoli to a bowl.

3. Wipe out the frying pan. Heat the oil over moderate heat. Add the garlic and cook, stirring frequently, just until golden brown, about 3 minutes. Using a slotted spoon, transfer the garlic to a paper towel to drain.

4. Add the broccoli to the pan, increase the heat to moderately high, and cook, tossing occasionally, until heated through, browned in spots, and crisp-tender, about 3 minutes. Season with salt and pepper.

Arrange the broccoli on a serving platter and scatter the garlic chips over the top.

—SUSAN SHAPIRO JASLOVE

BROCCOLI WITH BLACK OLIVES

When peeled and cut into pieces, broccoli stems can be transformed into a very tender vegetable. Here the stems and florets are tossed with butter and chopped black olives for a very simple but flavorful side dish.

SERVES 4

1 pound broccoli, cut into florets, stalks peeled and sliced 1 inch thick

2 tablespoons butter

12 Kalamata or other brine-cured black olives, pitted and chopped

Salt and fresh-ground black pepper

1. In a large pot of boiling, salted water cook the broccoli stems for 1 minute. Add the broccoli florets and cook until just tender, about 4 minutes. Drain well.

2. Return the broccoli to the pot and toss with the butter. Add the olives, season with salt and pepper, and toss again.

—SARAH FRITSCHNER

BROCCOLI RABE WITH ORECCHIETTE

Bright green broccoli rabe and red bell peppers combine to create this satisfying pasta side dish. Blanching the broccoli rabe in boiling water helps to tame its assertive but pleasantly bitter flavor.

SERVES 4

½ pound orecchiette

1½ tablespoons extra-virgin olive oil

6 cloves garlic, thinly sliced

1 large red bell pepper, cut into ⅓-inch dice

½ teaspoon dried red-pepper flakes

Salt

1¼ pounds broccoli rabe, tough stems removed and stalks cut into 1-inch lengths

1. In a large pot of boiling, salted water, cook the orecchiette, stirring occasionally, until just done, about 15 minutes. Drain well. Transfer to a serving bowl and keep warm.

2. Meanwhile, in a large heavy frying pan, heat the oil over moderate heat. Add the garlic, bell pepper, and red-pepper flakes and cook, stirring frequently, until the garlic is tender but not browned, 10 to 12 minutes. Stir in ½ teaspoon salt. Remove from the heat.

3. In a large pot of boiling water, cook the broccoli rabe until tender, 3 to 5 minutes. Drain well. Stir into the garlic mixture and reheat briefly if necessary. Season with additional salt if desired. Stir the vegetables into the pasta.

—DIANA STURGIS

229

SAUTEED BROCCOLI RABE WITH PARMESAN

Broccoli rabe looks like slender stalks of broccoli, bearing large jagged leaves and tiny florets at the head. The full flavor matches well with Parmesan cheese in this quick and easy side dish, which makes an excellent accompaniment to meat or poultry served with tomato sauce. If broccoli rabe is not available, use Swiss chard instead.

SERVES 4

1 tablespoon butter

1 tablespoon olive oil

1 pound broccoli rabe, tough stems removed and stalks cut into 3-inch lengths

   Salt and fresh-ground black pepper

3 tablespoons grated Parmesan cheese

1. Rinse the broccoli rabe and shake off the excess water.

2. In a large frying pan, melt the butter with the oil over moderate heat. Add the broccoli rabe with the water that clings to it, season with salt and pepper, and stir to coat. Cover and cook over high heat for 1 minute. Stir, reduce the heat to moderate, and cover. Cook until the broccoli rabe is crisp-tender, about 3 minutes.

3. Season with salt and pepper and sprinkle with the grated Parmesan.

—BOB CHAMBERS

Marinated Cucumbers

This simple, unusual, and particularly Tuscan dish was traditionally associated with the gathering of the grain at harvest time. The sweetened cucumbers were probably served as a palate refresher before the dessert course at the big festive dinner for all the neighbors who helped out. The dish was so well liked that it became a popular snack to have during a small rest break from work.

SERVES 6

- 2 English cucumbers, peeled and cut into ⅛-inch slices
- 2 tablespoons lemon juice
- ½ cup sugar

1. Put the cucumbers into a medium bowl. Drizzle the lemon juice over the top and sprinkle with the sugar. Do not mix. Cover and refrigerate for at least 2 hours or up to 24 hours.

2. Just before serving, toss well. Spoon the cucumbers and their juices into shallow bowls and serve cold.

—Giuliano Bugialli

ROASTED EGGPLANT WITH ARUGULA

The flavors of the Mediterranean come through in this warm salad that would be excellent served as a first course or as a side dish to grilled lamb chops or Italian sausages.

SERVES 4

5 tablespoons olive oil

1 small eggplant (about 1 pound), peeled, cut into 1-inch rounds, and each round cut into 4 strips

Salt and fresh-ground black pepper

2 tablespoons balsamic vinegar

¾ pound arugula, stems removed and leaves chopped (about 8 cups)

1. Heat the oven to 450°. Pour 2 tablespoons of the oil onto a baking sheet and dip the eggplant into the oil to coat. Season the strips with salt and pepper and spread out on the baking sheet. Roast the eggplant in the bottom third of the oven until tender and deep brown on the underside, about 25 minutes. Using a metal spatula, transfer the eggplant to a plate.

2. In a small bowl, whisk together the vinegar, ½ teaspoon salt, and ¼ teaspoon pepper. Add the remaining 3 tablespoons oil slowly, whisking.

3. In a large bowl, toss the arugula with 3 tablespoons of the dressing. Transfer the salad to a platter and arrange the roasted eggplant on top. Drizzle the eggplant with the remaining dressing.

—MARCIA KIESEL

FRESH FAVA BEANS WITH ESCAROLE AND TOMATO

In this hearty side dish, the vegetables are steamed separately and then cooked together briefly. When buying fava beans (also called broad beans), choose slender, bright green, fresh-looking pods; the beans will be small and sweet. Larger beans tend to be starchy.

SERVES 4

- 3 pounds fava beans, shelled
- 1 small head escarole, cut into 1-inch strips (about 3 packed cups)
- 1½ tablespoons olive oil
- 1 onion, thinly sliced
- 2 cloves garlic, crushed
- ½ teaspoon chopped fresh thyme, or a pinch dried
  Salt
- 1 tablespoon chopped flat-leaf parsley
- ½ cup water
- 1 tablespoon red-wine vinegar
  Fresh-ground black pepper
- 1 medium tomato, peeled, seeded, and cut into ¼-inch strips

1. Put the fava beans in a steamer basket set into a medium saucepan filled with 1 inch boiling water. Cover and steam until tender, 8 to 10 minutes. Transfer the fava beans to a plate to cool slightly.

2. Add the escarole to the steamer basket. Cover and steam for 3 minutes. Remove the escarole, drain off the water, and wipe the pan dry.

3. In the saucepan, combine the oil, onion, garlic, thyme, and ¼ teaspoon salt. Cover and cook over low heat for 5 minutes, stirring once or twice. Add the parsley and water and bring to a boil. Cover partially, reduce the heat, and simmer until the liquid has reduced to 2 tablespoons, about 5 minutes.

4. Meanwhile, peel the fava beans by splitting the tough skins with your thumbnail and popping out the tender beans. Add the beans, escarole, and vinegar to the pan. Toss gently and cook over low heat to blend the flavors and warm through, about 2 minutes. Season with salt and pepper. Remove from the heat and stir in the tomato. Serve warm or at room temperature.

—STEPHANIE LYNESS

BAKED FENNEL WITH PARMESAN

Fennel, or *finocchio* as it is known in Italy, is a favorite vegetable among Italians. It can be sliced paper-thin and served raw with a little olive oil drizzled over it, or cooked in a variety of ways. Baking makes the vegetable extra tender and mellows and sweetens its aniselike flavor.

SERVES 6

5 small fennel bulbs (about 3 pounds), cut into quarters

4 tablespoons butter

¼ teaspoon salt

½ teaspoon fresh-ground black pepper

⅓ cup Chicken Stock, page 79, or canned low-sodium chicken broth

¼ cup grated Parmesan cheese

1. Soak the fennel in cold water to cover for 20 minutes. Drain.

2. Heat the oven to 350°. In a large pot of boiling, salted water, cook the fennel for 5 minutes. Drain, rinse with cold water, and drain well.

3. Grease a large shallow baking dish with 1 tablespoon of the butter. Cut the remaining 3 tablespoons butter into small pieces. Layer half of the fennel in the dish, scatter the butter over the fennel, and season with ⅛ teaspoon of the salt and ¼ teaspoon of the pepper. Top with the remaining fennel, gently press down, and season with the remaining ⅛ teaspoon salt and ¼ teaspoon pepper.

4. Pour the stock over the fennel, cover with foil, and bake for 45 minutes. Increase the temperature to 400°. Uncover the fennel and bake until the liquid has evaporated, about 20 minutes longer. Sprinkle the Parmesan over the fennel and bake until golden, about 10 minutes.

—NANCY VERDE BARR

ROASTED FENNEL WITH ROSEMARY

Many Italians look forward to autumn because it brings with it an abundant supply of fennel. Roasting is an easy and delicious way to prepare fennel and it brings out its subtle, sweet flavor.

SERVES 4

2 large fennel bulbs, cut into 8 wedges each

6 shallots, halved lengthwise

1½ tablespoons butter, cut into small pieces

1½ tablespoons olive oil

2 teaspoons finely chopped fresh rosemary, or ½ teaspoon dried

1 teaspoon sugar

   Salt and fresh-ground black pepper

1 lemon wedge

1. Heat the oven to 350°. In a heavy medium casserole, toss the fennel with the shallots, butter, oil, rosemary, and sugar. Season with salt and pepper. Cover tightly and roast, stirring two or three times, until the fennel is tender, about 50 minutes.

2. Squeeze the lemon over the fennel and toss well.

—BRIGIT LEGERE BINNS

MAKE IT AHEAD

The roasted fennel can be refrigerated, covered, for up to a day. Gently reheat before adding the lemon juice and serving.

GREEN BEANS WITH OLIVE OIL AND GARLIC

The green beans that grow all over Italy are picked when they are quite young, still thin, and tender. They're frequently boiled first, then dressed simply with olive oil and lemon or sautéed with garlic and perhaps basil, anchovies, or anise seeds. Serve this dish with any grilled or broiled fish.

SERVES 4

1 pound green beans

1 cup flat-leaf parsley leaves

¼ cup fresh basil leaves

2 large cloves garlic

2 anchovy fillets

1 tablespoon butter

2 tablespoons olive oil

Salt and fresh-ground black pepper

1. Soak the green beans in a medium bowl in cold water to cover for 30 minutes. Drain.

2. In a large saucepan of boiling, salted water, cook the beans until just tender, about 5 minutes. Drain, rinse with cold water, and drain well.

3. Meanwhile, finely chop the parsley and basil with the garlic and anchovies. In a large frying pan, melt the butter with the oil over moderate heat. Add the parsley mixture and cook, stirring occasionally, until fragrant, about 5 minutes. Add the beans and toss until heated through, about 3 minutes. Season with salt and pepper.

—GIULIANO BUGIALLI

Green Beans with Balsamic-Glazed Onions

In this recipe, the natural sugar in balsamic vinegar caramelizes the pearl onions and adds a touch of sweetness to the mustard-vinegar sauce.

SERVES 4

1   pound pearl onions or one 16-ounce bag frozen pearl onions, thawed

¼   cup balsamic vinegar

1   tablespoon butter

1   tablespoon vegetable oil

1   teaspoon finely chopped fresh thyme

¾   teaspoon fresh-ground black pepper

1½   pounds green beans

2   tablespoons olive oil

1½   teaspoons Dijon mustard

½   teaspoon salt

1. In a large saucepan of boiling water, blanch the fresh onions, if using, for 1 minute. Drain, rinse with cold water, and drain well. Using a small sharp knife, trim the root ends and slip off the skins.

2. Heat the oven to 400°. In a small stainless-steel saucepan, combine 2 tablespoons of the balsamic vinegar, the butter, vegetable oil, thyme, and ¼ teaspoon of the pepper and stir over moderately low heat until the butter is melted. Transfer to a medium bowl, add the fresh or frozen onions, and toss to coat. Spread the onions in a single layer on a baking sheet and roast, stirring often, until evenly browned, 35 to 40 minutes.

3. Meanwhile, in a large pot of boiling, salted water, cook the green beans until tender, about 4 minutes. Drain, rinse with cold water, and drain well.

4. In a medium bowl, combine the olive oil, mustard, the remaining 2 tablespoons balsamic vinegar, the salt, and the remaining ½ teaspoon pepper.

5. Remove the onions from the oven and reduce the oven temperature to 350°. Add the green beans and onions to the dressing and toss well.

6. Transfer the vegetables to a large casserole. Cover and bake until heated through, about 20 minutes.

—Bob Chambers

Make It Ahead

The recipe can be prepared through step 5 up to a day ahead; cover the casserole and refrigerate. Return to room temperature before baking.

HERBED CARROTS AND GREEN BEANS

The subtle lemon and anchovy flavors of this dish go well with most baked, grilled, or broiled fish or chicken dishes. Carrots and green beans together make an especially attractive presentation, but you could opt for using just one of the vegetables instead.

SERVES 6

¼ pound butter

1 clove garlic, minced

¾ pound green beans, cut into 2-inch lengths

6 carrots, cut into 2 by ¼-inch julienne strips

3 tablespoons chopped flat-leaf parsley

2 teaspoons chopped fresh marjoram, or ½ teaspoon dried

1 teaspoon chopped fresh rosemary, or ¼ teaspoon dried

¼ teaspoon salt

¼ teaspoon fresh-ground black pepper

3 anchovy fillets, mashed

Grated zest of 1 lemon

2 teaspoons lemon juice

1. In a large frying pan, melt the butter over moderately low heat. Add the garlic and cook until lightly colored, about 2 minutes.

2. Add the beans, carrots, parsley, marjoram, rosemary, salt, and pepper. Toss to combine. Cover and cook, tossing occasionally, until the vegetables are just tender, 10 to 12 minutes. (If the vegetables begin to stick, add 1 to 2 tablespoons of water.)

3. Add the anchovies, lemon zest, and lemon juice. Cook, tossing occasionally, for 2 minutes.

—NANCY VERDE BARR

BRAISED MUSHROOMS WITH PANCETTA AND PINE NUTS

Pancetta can be very salty, so season this dish with discretion. If you cannot find pancetta, prosciutto is a good substitute.

SERVES 6

1 ounce dried porcini mushrooms

2 cups boiling water

2 to 4 tablespoons olive oil

¼ pound pancetta, cut into ⅛-inch dice

¼ cup pine nuts

1 small onion, minced

1 large clove garlic, minced

1 pound white mushrooms, thinly sliced

¼ cup dry Madeira or tawny port

2 tablespoons heavy cream

¼ cup minced flat-leaf parsley

Salt and fresh-ground black pepper

1. Put the dried porcini in a small bowl and pour the boiling water over them. Soak until softened, about 20 minutes. Remove the mushrooms, reserving the soaking liquid, and squeeze the mushrooms to remove as much liquid as possible. Coarsely chop. Strain the liquid through a paper-towel-lined sieve. Reserve ½ cup and discard the rest.

2. In a large frying pan, heat 2 tablespoons of the oil over moderately low heat. Add the pancetta and cook, stirring occasionally, until golden brown, 8 to 10 minutes. With a slotted spoon, transfer to a small bowl. Add additional oil if necessary to the fat in the skillet to measure 3 tablespoons.

3. Increase the heat to moderate, add the pine nuts, and toast, stirring frequently, until golden, about 3 minutes. Remove with the slotted spoon and add to the pancetta.

4. Reduce the heat to low, add the onion and garlic, and cook, stirring occasionally, until softened, 2 to 3 minutes.

5. Increase the heat to high, add the porcini and the fresh mushrooms, and cook, tossing occasionally, until the mushrooms begin to release their liquid, 5 to 7 minutes. Add the Madeira and the porcini soaking liquid and boil until the liquid is reduced to 2 tablespoons, about 5 minutes. Add the cream, reduce the heat to low, and cook until the sauce thickens slightly, about 2 minutes.

6. Stir in the parsley, pancetta, and pine nuts. Season with salt and pepper.

—NANCY VERDE BARR

GRILLED WILD MUSHROOM AND BREAD SKEWERS

Grilled vegetable skewers are a natural to serve with a grilled meat, poultry, or fish dish. Use shiitake mushrooms with thick fleshy caps for these skewers because they will tolerate the heat of grilling without overcooking.

SERVES 4

16   ¾-inch slices Italian bread

½   cup extra-virgin olive oil

3   cloves garlic, minced

1½   tablespoons finely chopped fresh rosemary, or 1½ teaspoons dried

1½   teaspoons finely chopped fresh sage, or ½ teaspoon dried

Salt and fresh-ground black pepper

12   shiitake mushrooms, about 2½ inches in diameter, stems removed

2   bunches arugula (about ¼ pound in all), stems discarded

2   teaspoons lemon juice, or to taste

1. Heat the oven to 250°. Put the bread on a baking sheet and toast in the oven for 10 minutes.

2. In a small bowl, combine 6 tablespoons of the oil with the garlic, rosemary, and sage. Season with salt and pepper. Lightly brush the mushroom caps and bread with the herb oil, stuffing the seasonings into the undersides of the mushrooms. Alternately thread 3 mushrooms and 4 slices of bread onto a metal skewer, beginning and ending with a bread slice. Thread another skewer next to the first skewer to secure the mushrooms and bread. Repeat with the remaining bread and mushrooms. Brush with any remaining herb oil.

3. Light a grill or heat the broiler. Lightly oil the grill or lightly oil a baking sheet and put the skewers on the baking sheet. Grill or broil the skewers for 3 to 5 minutes, turning, until golden brown on all sides.

4. In a medium bowl, toss the arugula with the remaining 2 tablespoons oil and the lemon juice. Season with salt and pepper. Serve the skewered bread and mushrooms with the arugula salad.

—VIANA LA PLACE

ROASTED ONIONS WITH RED PEPPERS AND GARLIC CROUTONS

These onions are wonderfully sweet and earthy, and their caramelized juices become the basis for the accompanying vinaigrette. Be sure to use a heavy roasting pan to keep the juices from evaporating during baking. In season, small sweet onions are best; otherwise, red onions work perfectly well. For the best results, choose well-shaped, unblemished onions.

SERVES 8

8   small sweet or red onions (about 3 ounces each)

3   large heads garlic

4   red bell peppers

    Coarse salt and fresh-ground black pepper

1   cup extra-virgin olive oil

1   tablespoon chopped fresh marjoram, stems reserved, or 2 teaspoons dried

2   teaspoons fresh thyme leaves, stems reserved, or 2 teaspoons dried

¼   cup Chicken Stock, page 79, or canned low-sodium chicken broth

1½ tablespoons balsamic vinegar

1   teaspoon Dijon mustard

8   ½-inch slices sourdough or other sturdy white bread

4   bunches lamb's lettuce (mâche)

1. Heat the oven to 350°. Cut off the root and stem ends of the onions. Remove any loose skin from the onions and heads of garlic, but do not peel.

2. Put the onions, garlic, and bell peppers in a large heavy roasting pan. Sprinkle with 1½ teaspoons salt and ½ teaspoon black pepper. Drizzle ¼ cup of the oil over the vegetables and toss to coat. Stand the onions and garlic bulbs on their root ends and lay the bell peppers on their sides, allowing about 1 inch between the vegetables. Roast for 30 minutes. Turn the onions and peppers over. Add the marjoram and thyme stems, or sprinkle 1 teaspoon each of the dried marjoram and thyme over the vegetables. Roast for 30 minutes longer.

3. Remove the peppers and garlic. Turn the onions over again, setting them in the same spots where the juices have caramelized (don't be alarmed by the blackness of the caramelized juices). Roast the onions until very soft and easily pierced with the tip of a long knife, about 20 minutes longer. Remove the pan from the oven, cover with foil, and set aside for 20 minutes.

4. Transfer the onions to a plate and let cool completely. Put the roasting pan over moderate heat and add the stock. Bring to a boil, scraping the bottom of the pan to dislodge the browned bits, and cook until the caramelized juices have dissolved and the

liquid is reduced by half, about 2 minutes. Strain the juices through a fine sieve into a medium bowl. Add the remaining 1 teaspoon each dried thyme and marjoram, if using, and let cool.

5. Working over a bowl to catch the juices, pull the skin off the peppers. Remove the stems, seeds, and ribs. Cut each pepper into 10 strips. Strain the pepper juices into the caramelized onion syrup.

6. Separate the garlic cloves and squeeze the pulp into a strainer set over a small bowl. Using a rubber spatula, press the garlic through the strainer.

7. In a small bowl, whisk together the vinegar, mustard, and 3 tablespoons of the garlic puree until smooth. Add ½ cup of the oil, slowly whisking, then whisk in the caramelized onion syrup. Whisk in 2 teaspoons of the fresh marjoram and the fresh thyme, if using. Season with salt and black pepper.

8. Heat the broiler. Lightly brush the bread slices on both sides with 2 tablespoons of the oil. Cut each slice into 4 triangles, place on a baking sheet, and broil, turning once, until lightly golden on both sides.

9. In a small bowl, combine the remaining garlic puree, 1 teaspoon fresh marjoram, if using, and 2 tablespoons olive oil. Season

with salt and black pepper. Spread a very thin layer of the garlic mixture on each crouton.

10. Discard the dry, leathery outer layers of the onions. Set the onions on a platter. Arrange the pepper strips, lettuce, and croutons around the onions. Whisk the vinaigrette and pass it separately.

—ANDREW ZIOBRO

Parmesan Mashed Potatoes

These mashed potatoes, made with just milk and Parmesan cheese, have lots of body. Look for yellow-fleshed Yukon Gold potatoes for this recipe. They have a wonderfully rich, buttery flavor and make fabulous mashed potatoes.

SERVES 4

1½   pounds Yukon Gold or boiling potatoes (about 6 medium), peeled and quartered

3   tablespoons grated Parmesan cheese

½   teaspoon salt

⅛   teaspoon fresh-ground black pepper

½   cup milk, heated

1. Put the potatoes in a medium saucepan of salted water. Bring to a boil, reduce the heat, and simmer until tender, about 20 minutes.

2. Drain the potatoes and put them back into the saucepan along with the cheese, salt, and pepper. Mash the potatoes over very low heat, gradually incorporating the milk and mashing until almost smooth.

—Tom Maresca and Diane Darrow

Parmigiano-Reggiano

Parmigiano-Reggiano is the highest-quality Parmesan cheese available, and to many, it is the only Parmesan. Its production is strictly limited to the provinces of Parma, Reggio Emilia, Modena, Mantova, and Bologna.

On April 1, production begins with the milk from cows that have fed in fresh pastures, and it ends promptly on November 11. Parmigiano-Reggiano is made completely by hand in an artisan's tradition that is hundreds of years old. It is aged for at least two years, and usually longer.

To distinguish Parmigiano-Reggiano from other lesser-quality Parmesans, small dots spelling out its name are etched around the entire circumference of the 60- to 70-pound wheels.

When buying Parmigiano-Reggiano for grating, look for a faintly moist, straw-yellow chunk that crumbles softly in your hand. It should taste mellow but rich and minimally salty, with a slightly sweet aftertaste. If you want to serve Parmesan as an eating cheese, look for a younger, less-yellow, moister wedge.

GREMOLATA CRUSHED POTATOES

Garlic, parsley, and lemon zest, chopped together to make the garnish known as gremolata, give these mashed potatoes lots of zesty flavor. Leaving the skins on the potatoes adds texture and color.

SERVES 6

2 pounds small red potatoes, quartered

1 small lemon

1 cup (loosely packed) flat-leaf parsley leaves

1 clove garlic

¼ pound butter, at room temperature

1 teaspoon coarse salt

1. Put the potatoes in a medium saucepan of salted water. Bring to a boil, reduce the heat, and simmer until tender, about 15 minutes.

2. Meanwhile, using a vegetable peeler, remove the zest of the lemon in strips, taking care not to include any of the bitter white pith. On a cutting board, finely chop the zest with the parsley and garlic to make the gremolata.

3. Drain the potatoes and put them back into the saucepan. Very coarsely mash the potatoes over very low heat, gradually incorporating the butter. Stir in the salt and half the gremolata. Transfer to a serving bowl and sprinkle with the remaining gremolata.

—GEORGE GERMON AND JOHANNE KILLEEN, AL FORNO, PROVIDENCE, RHODE ISLAND

PAN-GRILLED RADICCHIO WITH ANCHOVY-MUSTARD SAUCE

Vivid garnet heads of radicchio reveal an intriguing bitter flavor when grilled. The tastiest radicchio is the Treviso variety, with long, narrow heads shaped like loose-leafed Belgian endive. Round-headed Verona radicchio, which resembles baby red cabbage, isn't as flavorful, but this recipe works well with either variety. It is good served with grilled chicken or fish, either as a side dish or as a warm salad after the main course.

SERVES 4 TO 6

2 anchovy fillets

1 tablespoon Dijon mustard

¼ cup lemon juice

1 clove garlic, lightly crushed

1 tablespoon minced flat-leaf parsley

½ teaspoon dried rosemary

½ cup extra-virgin olive oil

4 small heads radicchio (1 to 1¼ pounds), outer leaves removed, quartered lengthwise, with ends intact

Salt and fresh-ground black pepper

1. In a small bowl, mash the anchovies to a paste. Whisk in the mustard, lemon juice, garlic, parsley, and rosemary. Add 6 tablespoons of the oil slowly, whisking.

2. Heat a very large cast-iron frying pan or griddle over moderate heat. Brush the radicchio with the remaining 2 tablespoons oil and lay them in the pan or on the griddle. Season with salt and pepper. Cook, turning, until the radicchio is lightly browned and tender, about 8 minutes.

3. Arrange the grilled radicchio on a serving plate, cut-sides up. Stir the mustard sauce, discard the garlic, and spoon the sauce over the radicchio. Serve warm or at room temperature.

—TOM MARESCA AND DIANE DARROW

SPINACH AND ROASTED RED PEPPER GRATIN

This dish would be excellent served with roasted or grilled chicken or beef. Spinach and roasted red pepper, blended with a light custard, are transformed into a gratin with a golden Parmesan and bread crumb topping.

SERVES 8

1   large red bell pepper

6   pounds spinach, stems removed and leaves washed

2   teaspoons extra-virgin olive oil

2   large eggs

⅔   cup skim milk

5   cloves garlic, minced

2   teaspoons chopped fresh thyme, or 1 teaspoon dried

1½ teaspoons salt

¾   teaspoon fresh-ground black pepper

3   tablespoons fresh or dry bread crumbs

2   tablespoons grated Parmesan cheese

1. Roast the pepper over an open flame or broil, turning with tongs, until charred all over, about 10 minutes. When the pepper is cool enough to handle, pull off the skin. Working over a large bowl to catch the juices, remove the stem, seeds, and ribs. Cut the pepper into ¼-inch strips.

2. In a large pot of boiling, salted water, blanch the spinach in batches just until wilted. Using a slotted spoon, remove the wilted spinach to a bowl of cold water. Drain. Squeeze the spinach to remove as much liquid as possible, then coarsely chop.

3. Coat a 10-inch round glass or ceramic baking dish with ½ teaspoon of the oil. Beat the eggs and skim milk into the roasted red pepper liquid. Stir in the spinach, garlic, thyme, salt, and black pepper. Spoon the mixture into the prepared dish and sprinkle the bread crumbs and Parmesan over the top. Arrange the bell pepper strips over the top in a starburst pattern and drizzle with the remaining 1½ teaspoons oil.

4. Bake the gratin until heated through and lightly browned, about 30 minutes. Let cool slightly, then cut into wedges and serve warm.

—MARTHA ROSE SHULMAN

Spinach with Raisins and Pine Nuts

In the spring, Italians enjoy fresh, tender spinach either in salad with a drizzle of extra-virgin olive oil and fresh lemon juice, or sautéed with raisins and pine nuts, as here.

SERVES 4

½ cup raisins

2 pounds spinach, with stems

2 tablespoons extra-virgin olive oil

Salt

¼ cup pine nuts

1. Put the raisins in a small bowl, pour 1 cup of warm water over them and set aside for 30 minutes. Drain well.

2. In a large pot, bring about 1 cup of salted water to a boil over high heat. Stir in the spinach and cook, stirring, until it is just wilted, about 2 minutes.

3. Drain the spinach and rinse with cold water. When the spinach is cool enough to handle, squeeze out the excess liquid.

4. In a large frying pan, heat the oil over moderate heat. Add the spinach and raisins and cook, stirring, until heated through, about 5 minutes. Season with salt.

5. Arrange the spinach mixture on a platter and sprinkle with the pine nuts.

—Lorenza de'Medici

Pine Nuts

Pine nuts, also known as *pignoli* and *piñon*, are found in the pine cones of certain varieties of pine trees. Rich and creamy, they used to be served in Liguria during Lent, when most foods of substance, including meat and cheese, were forbidden. Pine nuts are often used to flavor sweet breads and dessert fillings; meat dishes, particularly game; and sweet-and-sour sauces such as caponata. Because they are individually extracted and shelled, they are considerably more expensive than most other nuts.

GARLICKY SPINACH

The beauty of this easy side dish is that it can be enjoyed with almost any meal, any time of the year. Fruity olive oil coats the spinach leaves with garlic and shallots to heighten the flavor. Be sure to wash the spinach leaves well to remove all the sand and grit. The best way to do this is to fill the sink with tepid water and submerge the spinach in the water. Slosh it around, then lift it out to a colander to drain.

SERVES 6

4 pounds spinach, stems removed

2 tablespoons extra-virgin olive oil

2 cloves garlic, minced

1 large shallot, finely chopped

Salt and fresh-ground black pepper

1. Rinse the spinach but do not dry. Tear any large leaves in half.

2. In a large stainless-steel pot, heat the oil over moderate heat. Add the garlic and shallot and cook, stirring frequently, until softened. Add the spinach with the water that is still clinging to its leaves. Cover and cook until the spinach is wilted, about 2 minutes. Season with salt and pepper.

—BRIGIT LEGERE BINNS

GRATIN OF TOMATOES AND GRILLED PEPPERS WITH ROASTED POLENTA

This hearty vegetable dish is full of flavor and can be served as a side or main course. The gratin is beautiful served with wedges of roasted polenta alongside.

SERVES 4

2   cups water

½   cup instant polenta

Salt and fresh-ground black pepper

1   tablespoon butter

2   red bell peppers

2   yellow bell peppers

3   to 4 tablespoons extra-virgin olive oil

2   small cloves garlic, sliced paper thin

4   anchovy fillets, cut into small pieces

½   teaspoon dried red-pepper flakes

1½ pounds plum tomatoes (about 7), peeled, seeded, and coarsely chopped

¼   cup chopped flat-leaf parsley

12 small fresh green or purple basil leaves

1. Oil an 8-inch pie pan. In a medium saucepan, bring the water to a boil. Add the polenta in a slow stream, whisking constantly. Reduce the heat to very low and cook, stirring constantly with a wooden spoon, until the polenta is very thick and pulls away from the sides of the pan, 4 to 5 minutes. Season with salt and black pepper and stir in the butter. Pour into the prepared pan and let cool.

2. Roast the bell peppers directly over an open flame or broil, turning with tongs, until charred all over, about 10 minutes. When cool enough to handle, pull off the skins. Remove the stems, seeds, and ribs. Cut the peppers into ¾-inch strips.

3. Heat the oven to 400°. Oil a 9-inch gratin dish. Arrange a layer of the roasted peppers in the bottom of the dish. Sprinkle with a little of the garlic, anchovies, red-pepper flakes, and season with salt. Scatter some of the tomatoes over the top, sprinkle with parsley, and season again with a little salt. Moisten with a few drops of the oil. Continue layering the ingredients in this way, ending with a layer of peppers. Drizzle the remaining oil over the top and bake for 20 minutes. Remove from the oven and cover tightly to keep warm.

4. Heat the broiler. Lightly oil a small baking sheet. Unmold the polenta, cut into 4 wedges, and put on the baking sheet. Broil, turning once, until browned at the edges, about 5 minutes per side.

5. Transfer the polenta to 4 plates. Arrange the peppers and tomatoes alongside and drizzle a big spoonful of the cooking juices over them. Garnish with the basil.

—VIANA LA PLACE

FALL VEGETABLE SPIEDINI

This dish has all the bright colors of fall with rich flavor to match. Serve hot off the grill with piping-hot, soft polenta that has been enriched with cream or mascarpone.

SERVES 4

½ pound butternut squash, peeled, seeded, and cut into 1-inch chunks

16 pearl onions, preferably red, unpeeled

1 red bell pepper, cut into 1-inch squares

1 green bell pepper, cut into 1-inch squares

16 cremini mushrooms, stems removed

3 zucchini, cut into 1-inch chunks

¼ cup extra-virgin olive oil

2 teaspoons chopped fresh thyme, or ½ teaspoon dried

2 teaspoons chopped fresh rosemary, or ½ teaspoon dried

2 cloves garlic, thinly sliced

Salt and fresh-ground black pepper

1. In a medium saucepan of boiling water, cook the squash until just tender, about 3 minutes. Using a slotted spoon, remove the squash and drain well. Add the onions to the boiling water and cook until just tender, 2 to 4 minutes. Drain and peel them.

2. In a large bowl, combine the squash, onions, bell peppers, mushrooms, and zucchini. Drizzle with the oil. Add the thyme, rosemary, and garlic, and season with salt and pepper. Toss well. Set aside at room temperature for at least 1 hour.

3. Light a grill or heat the broiler. Thread the vegetables onto 8 metal skewers, alternating them in contrasting colors. Grill or broil, turning often, until the vegetables are tender and golden, about 5 minutes; brush the vegetables with a little oil if they start to dry out. Serve hot or at room temperature.

—VIANA LA PLACE

FRIED ZUCCHINI

A garden without an abundance of zucchini could hardly be called Italian. This is one of the many ways Italians prepare this popular vegetable. The secret to frying foods successfully is the temperature of the oil—it should be hot, but not so hot that it smokes and burns the food. Test the oil by dropping in a small cube of bread: If it browns in about 1 minute, it is ready. Serve fried zucchini as a side dish with fish or chicken or as part of an antipasto selection.

SERVES 6

- 1 large egg
- ½ cup all-purpose flour
- ¼ teaspoon salt

  About ⅓ cup water
- 3 cups olive oil
- 3 zucchini (about 1½ pounds), cut into ⅛-inch slices

1. In a small bowl, lightly whisk the egg. Gradually sift in the flour and salt, whisking until smooth. Slowly whisk in the water. The mixture should be the consistency of thin pancake batter. Set aside to rest for at least 20 minutes.

2. In a large deep frying pan or deep-fryer, heat the oil over moderately high heat to 375°. One by one, dip the zucchini slices into the batter, shaking gently to release any excess. Slide into the hot oil and fry in small batches, turning, until golden, 1 to 3 minutes. Remove with a slotted spoon and drain on paper towels. Sprinkle with salt and serve immediately.

—Nancy Verde Barr

254

ZUCCHINI WITH FRESH THYME

This is a great side dish for a buffet. The recipe can easily be doubled and is just as flavorful at room temperature as it is when served hot.

SERVES 6

- ¼ cup extra-virgin olive oil
- 2 tablespoons unsalted butter
- ⅓ cup finely chopped onion
- ⅓ cup chopped fresh parsley
- 1½ pounds zucchini, soaked in water for 20 minutes, patted dry, and cut into 3 by ½-inch sticks
- 1 beef bouillon cube, crumbled
- 2 teaspoons chopped fresh thyme
  Salt and fresh-ground black pepper

1. In a large frying pan, combine the oil, butter, onion, and parsley. Cook over moderate heat, stirring occasionally, until the onion is softened but not browned, about 5 minutes.

2. Add the zucchini, bouillon cube, thyme, and a pinch each of salt and pepper. Stir gently but thoroughly, cover, and cook, stirring occasionally, until the zucchini is tender, 20 to 30 minutes. Serve hot or warm.

—PATRICIA WELLS

ZUCCHINI AND CARROTS PARMESAN

Mild flavored zucchini is endlessly versatile. Here it is shredded with sweet carrots for a simple and colorful side dish that takes only about 15 minutes to prepare. This would go well with broiled meats or fish.

SERVES 4

½ cup Chicken Stock, page 79, or canned low-sodium chicken broth

1 pound zucchini, shredded

2 carrots, shredded

Salt and fresh-ground pepper

1 tablespoon grated Parmesan cheese

1. In a medium frying pan, bring the chicken stock to a boil over moderately high heat and boil until reduced by half, about 2 minutes.

2. Add the zucchini and carrots and season with salt and pepper. Cook, stirring frequently, until the vegetables are just tender, about 4 minutes. Season with more salt and pepper if necessary, transfer to a serving dish, and sprinkle the Parmesan on top.

—MICHELE SCICOLONE

ROASTED VEGETABLES WITH PROSCIUTTO

Potatoes, onions, and red bell peppers roasted with prosciutto and fresh rosemary makes an easy and flavorful side dish. It would be a marvelous accompaniment to roasted or grilled meats, such as an herbed leg of lamb, steaks, or Italian sausages.

SERVES 6

1½ pounds boiling potatoes (about 3 medium), peeled and cut into ½-inch slices

2 onions, each cut into 8 wedges

4 red bell peppers, cut into thick slices

¼ pound thinly sliced prosciutto, shredded

1 teaspoon finely chopped fresh rosemary, or ½ teaspoon dried

½ teaspoon salt

¼ teaspoon fresh-ground black pepper

¼ cup extra-virgin olive oil

1. Heat the oven to 400°. Put the potatoes, onions, and bell peppers into a large roasting pan. Add the prosciutto, rosemary, salt, and black pepper. Drizzle with the oil and toss to coat the vegetables.

2. Roast the vegetables, stirring two or three times, until the potatoes are tender, about 35 minutes.

—NANCY VERDE BARR

DESSERTS

Hazelnut Biscotti with Black Pepper, 288

RAISINS SOAKED IN GRAPPA

These raisins will keep for at least six months, so prepare several jars. The raisins absorb almost all the grappa as they sit, until they are barely covered. Dried apricots and prunes can also be conserved in this manner and are delicious served either separately or mixed together. Of course, the success of this recipe depends on the quality of the grappa used.

SERVES 12

¾ cup golden raisins

1 cup grappa

1 clove

1. Put the raisins into a small glass jar and pour in the grappa. Add the clove and cover with a lid. Store at room temperature for at least 2 weeks before serving.

2. To serve, discard the clove, spoon the raisins into individual tumblers or small cups, and serve with demitasse spoons.

—LORENZA DE'MEDICI

GRAPPA

Grappa is brandy (technically, pomace brandy), and is distilled from the solids left after the fermentation of wine. Every winemaking region and town in Italy is therefore capable of making a distinctive grappa, and right now it appears as if they are all doing so.

After a big meal, grappa is one of the great, soothing palatal pleasures. Unaged grappa—readily identifiable by its crystal clarity—should be served ice cold in a pony glass; the chill tames its fire and releases its aroma. Don't serve grappa over ice. Instead, chill the whole bottle in the freezer for about an hour.

A wood-aged grappa can range in color from pale gold to deep amber. It should be served at room temperature in a brandy snifter, the better to savor its perfume. Treat grappa just as you would any fine brandy: sip it slowly, roll it over your tongue, savor, and enjoy.

—TOM MARESCA

Melon Sorbet with Port

Except on holidays and special occasions, Italians rarely end a meal with a rich dessert. Fruit, in one form or another, is usually on the after-dinner menu. Cantaloupe and port, a classic summertime pairing, combined with a touch of fresh-ground black pepper, makes a refreshing sorbet. It also works well as an intermezzo, a palate-refresher served between the first and main course.

MAKES ABOUT 3½ CUPS

2 small ripe cantaloupes

¼ cup sugar

1 tablespoon lemon juice

Pinch salt

½ teaspoon fresh-ground black pepper

Ruby port, chilled

1. Working on a large platter to catch the juices, halve and seed the cantaloupes. Peel and cut into chunks. Strain the juices into a 1-cup glass measure.

2. Add enough water to the cantaloupe juice to equal ¼ cup. Pour into a small heavy saucepan and add the sugar. Bring slowly to a boil, stirring to dissolve the sugar, and boil for 1 minute. Remove from the heat and let cool.

3. In a food processor or blender, puree the melon with the sugar syrup, lemon juice, salt, and pepper. Strain the mixture through a sieve (to prevent the sorbet from being grainy, do not press on the solids).

4. Pour the mixture into an ice-cream maker and freeze according to the manufacturer's instructions. Scoop into individual glasses and pour about 1 tablespoon of port on top of each serving.

—Enoteca Pinchiorri, Florence, Italy

RICOTTA GELATO

Nothing beats this rich and creamy ricotta ice cream flavored with pure vanilla, grappa-soaked raisins, and candied citrus peel.

MAKES ABOUT 2 QUARTS

1 cup golden raisins

¼ cup grappa or other brandy

2½ cups light cream or half-and-half

1 vanilla bean, split lengthwise, or 1½ teaspoons vanilla extract

1 tablespoon grated lemon zest

9 large egg yolks

1½ cups sugar

2 cups (about 1 pound) whole-milk ricotta

1 cup heavy cream

1 tablespoon chopped candied orange peel

1 tablespoon chopped candied lemon peel

1. In a medium saucepan, combine the raisins and grappa. Bring to a simmer over moderate heat. Remove from the heat, cover, and set aside for 1 to 2 hours. Drain.

2. Meanwhile, in a large heavy saucepan, combine the light cream, vanilla bean, if using, and lemon zest. Bring to a simmer over moderately high heat. Immediately remove from the heat, cover, and set aside.

3. In a large bowl, using an electric mixer, beat the egg yolks until pale yellow and fluffy. Gradually beat in the sugar. Continue beating until the mixture is thick enough to form a ribbon when the beaters are lifted.

4. Remove the vanilla bean, if using, from the hot cream mixture. Gradually whisk the cream into the egg-yolk mixture.

5. Pour the custard into a large heavy saucepan. Cook over low heat, stirring constantly, until the mixture thickens just enough to coat a spoon, about 15 minutes. Do not allow the custard to boil, or it may curdle.

6. Strain the custard into a bowl and let cool. Stir in the vanilla extract, if using. Cover and refrigerate until cold.

7. Put a 2-quart container into the freezer to chill. In a large bowl, beat together the ricotta and heavy cream until smooth. Stir into the cold custard. Pour the mixture into an ice-cream maker and freeze according to the manufacturer's instructions until almost frozen. Add the orange and lemon peels and raisins and freeze. Transfer the ice cream to the chilled container and store in the freezer for at least 3 hours. Let soften slightly at room temperature before serving.

—ALLEGRO, WALTHAM, MASSACHUSETTS

STRAWBERRY SHERBET WITH CHERRY-CARAMEL SAUCE

When preparing the caramel for this recipe, it is important to use a saucepan with sides high enough so that the foam that is created doesn't spill over.

MAKES ABOUT 1 QUART

- 1 pound bing cherries, pitted, or one 17-ounce can pitted black cherries in syrup
- 2 cups sugar
- ⅔ cup water
- 3 pounds (about 3 pints) strawberries, hulled
- 2 tablespoons lemon juice
- ½ cup orange liqueur, such as Grand Marnier

1. In a medium saucepan, combine the fresh cherries, if using, with 2 tablespoons of water and cook over low heat, covered, until softened, about 20 minutes. Puree the cherries in a food processor. If using canned cherries, put them into the processor with their syrup and puree.

2. In a heavy medium saucepan, combine 1 cup of the sugar with the water. Bring to a boil over high heat, swirling the pan, until the sugar is dissolved, 2 to 3 minutes. Let cool slightly.

3. Reserve a few of the smallest strawberries for garnish. Put the remaining strawberries in a food processor and pour in the cooled sugar syrup. Add the lemon juice and puree until smooth.

4. Put a serving bowl in the freezer to chill. Transfer the sherbet mixture to an ice-cream maker and freeze according to the manufacturer's instructions. Transfer the sherbet to the chilled bowl and keep, covered, in the freezer until ready to serve.

5. In a heavy medium saucepan, cook the remaining 1 cup sugar over moderate heat, swirling the pan, until the sugar melts. Bring to a boil and boil without stirring, until the caramel is dark gold and registers 240° on a candy thermometer, 15 to 16 minutes.

6. Standing back, add the liqueur a little at a time, stirring constantly with a long spoon until any lumps of caramel dissolve, about 1 minute. Be careful; the caramel will bubble up. Stir in the cherry puree and remove from the heat. Let cool to room temperature.

7. Pour the caramel sauce over the sherbet and garnish with the reserved strawberries. Serve immediately.

—Lorenza de'Medici

COFFEE SEMIFREDDO

Semifreddo al caffè, as this smooth, rich frozen mousse is called, is a snap to prepare. Since it's completely prepared ahead, it is especially suitable for entertaining.

SERVES 8

4 large egg yolks

½ cup sugar

2 cups heavy cream, chilled

2 tablespoons instant espresso powder

Whipped cream and grated semisweet chocolate, for garnish

1. In a medium bowl, using an electric mixer, beat the egg yolks on high speed until smooth. Gradually add the sugar and beat until thick and lemon-colored, 2 to 3 minutes.

2. In a large bowl, beat the cream until it holds soft peaks when the beaters are lifted. Sprinkle the espresso powder over the cream and fold in gently just until mixed.

3. Stir one quarter of the cream into the egg mixture to lighten it. Fold in the remaining cream just until combined. Spoon the mixture into eight 4-ounce ramekins. Cover loosely with plastic wrap and freeze until firm but not hard, 1 to 1½ hours.

4. To serve, garnish with whipped cream and grated chocolate.

—BETTE DUKE

SEMIFREDDO

A luscious cream-and-egg based Italian dessert, semifreddo has a consistency similar to that of a frozen mousse. The literal translation of *semifreddo* is "half frozen." In Italy, the word is used with abandon to describe many similar desserts. The flavorings also vary widely and include seasonal fresh berries such as raspberries or strawberries, coffee, lemon, crushed and toasted nuts, bananas, and chocolate.

ESPRESSO GRANITA

Granita di caffè is undoubtedly the most popular granita in Italy. The bitter-sweet taste of the icy espresso granules topped with softly whipped cream makes a refreshing substitute for "dessert and coffee" on a hot summer's day. (If you are sensitive to caffeine, use decaffeinated espresso beans.) For a little variety, add a dash of rum, brandy, or vanilla extract or a pinch of ground cinnamon to the mixture before freezing.

MAKES ABOUT 1½ QUARTS

¾ cup ground espresso beans

⅓ cup sugar

1 cup heavy cream

1. In an espresso maker or drip coffeepot, brew the coffee with 4 cups of water according to the manufacturer's directions. Add the sugar and stir until dissolved. Let cool slightly, then cover and refrigerate until cold.

2. Pour the coffee into a 13 by 9-inch metal pan. Freeze until ice crystals begin to form around the edges, about 30 minutes. Stir well and return the pan to the freezer. Continue freezing, stirring every 30 minutes, until the granita is completely frozen, about 2 to 2½ hours.

3. In a medium bowl, using an electric mixer, beat the cream until it holds soft peaks when the beaters are lifted. Scoop the granita into serving bowls and top with the whipped cream.

—MICHELE SCICOLONE

GRANITA

Granita is a cool and refreshing water-based ice frozen into grainy crystals, hence its name. It is the simplest of frozen desserts. Some historians say that granita was enjoyed by the ancient Romans, who sent runners to the nearby mountains for snow, which they flavored with honey, wine, fruit syrups, or herbs.

Granitas do not require churning, as ice cream does; the only equipment you need is a shallow metal pan and a fork. It does require frequent stirring during the freezing, though, to produce the grainy crystals.

To serve granita, use a metal spoon or fork to scrape across the surface of the granita, transferring the ice shards to chilled dessert glasses or wine goblets without packing the dessert down.

—MICHELE SCICOLONE

MINT GRANITA

Intensely flavored and palate-cleansing, this lovely and rather sophisticated ice would be especially refreshing after a meal featuring fish. You can use almost any mint leaves here, including peppermint, spearmint, or apple mint.

MAKES ABOUT 1½ QUARTS

4 cups water

¾ cup sugar

Leaves from 2 bunches fresh peppermint or spearmint, coarsely chopped (about 2 cups packed)

¼ cup lemon juice

1. In a medium saucepan, bring the water and sugar to a simmer over moderate heat. Cook until the sugar is completely dissolved, about 2 minutes. Stir in the mint, remove from the heat, and let cool. Cover and refrigerate until chilled.

2. Strain the mint syrup and discard the mint. Stir in the lemon juice. Pour into a 13 by 9-inch metal pan. Freeze until ice crystals begin to form around the edges, about 30 minutes. Stir well and return to the freezer. Continue freezing, stirring every 30 minutes, until the granita is completely frozen, about 2 to 2½ hours.

—MICHELE SCICOLONE

TIRAMISU

In Italy, this pudding-like dessert—which literally means "pick me up," probably because it is so tempting—was devised as a way to use up leftover cake or biscuits. Tiramisu by its very nature is an improvisational dessert that has many variations. However, it is almost always made with mascarpone cheese—the thick, fresh, naturally sweet Italian cream cheese. In this version, the dessert is made in individual portions using biscotti and topped with sweet, frothy zabaglione.

SERVES 6 TO 8

1   pound (2 cups) mascarpone cheese

¼   cup granulated sugar

2   tablespoons rum

24   biscotti all'uovo* or champagne biscuits

1   cup fresh-brewed espresso, cooled

4   large egg yolks

¼   cup superfine sugar

6   tablespoons sweet Marsala

2   tablespoons unsweetened cocoa powder
     Strawberries, for garnish

*Available at Italian and specialty food stores

1. Put the mascarpone, granulated sugar, and rum into a food processor and process until smooth.

2. On a serving plate, arrange 6 biscotti, flat-side up, side-by-side. Moisten lightly with ⅓ cup of the espresso. Spread one third of the cheese mixture over the biscotti. Repeat the layers two more times.

3. Halve the remaining 6 biscotti crosswise and use them to make a fence around the layered cheese.

4. In a medium bowl, whisk the egg yolks and superfine sugar until pale yellow and fluffy. Set the bowl over a large saucepan filled with 1 inch of simmering water. Using a hand-held electric mixer or the whisk, beat in the Marsala 1 tablespoon at a time, and continue to beat until the mixture is hot and thickened to the consistency of a light, fluffy batter. Immediately remove the zabaglione from the heat and beat for 3 minutes longer.

5. Spoon the zabaglione over the top of the dessert. Sprinkle the cocoa over the top. Garnish with strawberries.

—MARGARET AND G. FRANCO ROMAGNOLI

ORANGES WITH SWEET BASIL ZABAGLIONE

Traditionally, zabaglione is made with Marsala, but here the frothy custard sauce is flavored with white wine and fresh basil, making it a wonderful topping for juicy sweet oranges.

SERVES 4

8 large navel oranges

5 sprigs fresh basil, plus ½ cup (packed) fresh basil leaves, minced

2 large egg yolks

2 tablespoons sugar

¼ cup dry white wine

1. Remove a strip of zest from 1 of the oranges. Chop enough zest to measure ¼ teaspoon. Using a knife, peel all the oranges; cut in between the membranes to remove the sections.

2. Using your hands, lightly crush the basil sprigs. Toss in a large bowl with the orange sections. Cover and refrigerate for at least 2 hours but no longer than 6.

3. In a medium bowl, combine the egg yolks, sugar, wine, and orange zest. Set the bowl over a saucepan filled with 1 inch of simmering water and whisk until the zabaglione is frothy, thick, and doubled in volume, about 5 minutes. Stir in the minced basil.

4. Drain the orange sections and discard the basil. Divide the fruit among four bowls and spoon a heaping tablespoon of zabaglione over each.

—MARCIA KIESEL

ZABAGLIONE

Light and airy, made in only minutes, zabaglione is a perfect spur-of-the-moment dessert. The velvety, frothy custard is prepared from only three ingredients—eggs, sugar, and Marsala—beaten for 10 to 15 minutes over heat until thick and quadrupled in volume. The gossamer texture of the whipped custard and the heady perfume of the hot wine make it a favorite Italian dessert.

While this dessert is most often enjoyed warm by itself in large glass dishes, it can also be cooled quickly and spooned as a sauce over fruit. It is not stable enough to keep, however, and should be served immediately.

MOLDED RICOTTA AND MASCARPONE WITH STRAWBERRIES

In this simple yet luxurious dessert, ricotta and mascarpone cheeses are beaten until fluffy, then folded into whipped cream. It is particularly pretty when molded in a heart-shaped form, such as a *coeur à la crème* mold.

SERVES 6

1 envelope unflavored gelatin

⅓ cup plus 3 tablespoons orange liqueur

½ pound (about 1 cup) ricotta cheese, preferably fresh

½ pound (1 cup) mascarpone cheese

½ cup confectioners' sugar, sifted

1 teaspoon vanilla extract

1 tablespoon plus 1 teaspoon lemon juice

Pinch salt

½ cup heavy cream

1 pint strawberries, hulled and sliced, plus whole strawberries, for garnish

¼ cup raspberry jam

Fresh mint leaves, for garnish

1. Line a 1-quart mold or bowl with plastic wrap. In a small saucepan, sprinkle the gelatin over ⅓ cup of the liqueur and let stand until softened, about 5 minutes. Set the saucepan over low heat and stir until the gelatin dissolves, 2 to 3 minutes. Let cool slightly.

2. In a large bowl, using an electric mixer, beat the ricotta and mascarpone until smooth. Beat in the confectioners' sugar, vanilla, 1 teaspoon of the lemon juice, and the salt. Beat in the cooled gelatin mixture.

3. In a small bowl, beat the cream until it holds stiff peaks when the beaters are lifted. Fold the whipped cream into the cheese mixture. Pour into the prepared mold. Smooth the top and refrigerate until chilled and set, about 3 hours.

4. In a blender or food processor, puree ½ cup of the sliced strawberries with the jam. Strain the sauce and stir in the remaining 1 tablespoon lemon juice and 3 tablespoons orange liqueur. Add the remaining sliced berries.

5. Unmold the dessert onto a serving plate and surround it with the strawberry sauce. Garnish with strawberries and mint leaves.

—NANCY VERDE BARR

s

fl
e
a I
i
o ly
c

p
s

CHOCOLATE AND PISTACHIO CANNOLI

These cannoli take a bit of effort to prepare, but nothing can match the taste of a freshly made cannoli filled with chocolate cream. The chocolate cannoli dough is quite soft and should be kept as cool as possible during shaping and rolling.

MAKES ABOUT 20 CANNOLI

2 cups flour

½ cup plus 3 tablespoons unsweetened cocoa powder

1½ cups granulated sugar

4 tablespoons unsalted butter, at room temperature

1 cup dry Marsala

4 cups vegetable oil

1 large egg, beaten with 1 teaspoon water

1 cup heavy cream

⅔ cup plus 1 tablespoon ricotta cheese

⅔ cup raisins, chopped

3½ ounces unsalted shelled pistachios, toasted and finely chopped

3½ ounces semisweet chocolate, finely chopped

Confectioners' sugar, for dusting

1. In a large bowl, combine the flour, cocoa, and 6 tablespoons plus 2 teaspoons of the granulated sugar. Add the butter and Marsala and stir until a soft dough forms. Cover and refrigerate for 15 minutes.

2. Divide the dough into thirds. Work with one piece at a time, keeping the remaining dough refrigerated. On a well-floured surface, sprinkle the dough with flour and roll out ¼ inch thick. With a 3½-inch cookie cutter, stamp out rounds. Reserve the scraps. Roll the rounds into oval shapes; transfer to a baking sheet and refrigerate until ready to mold. Repeat with the remaining dough. Gather the scraps together and repeat to make more ovals.

3. In a deep medium saucepan or deep fryer, heat the oil to 350°. Wrap the ovals around cannoli forms, sealing the seams with the beaten egg. Fry the cannoli shells in batches until golden brown, about 2 minutes. Transfer to a rack to cool slightly, then remove the cannoli forms and repeat with the remaining ovals.

4. In a medium bowl, beat the cream just until it holds firm peaks when the beaters are lifted. In a large bowl, combine the ricotta and the remaining 1 cup plus 4 teaspoons granulated sugar. Stir in the raisins, pistachios, and chocolate. Fold in the whipped cream. Cover and refrigerate until ready to use.

5. Using a pastry bag or a small spoon, fill the cannoli shells with the ricotta mixture. Just before serving, dust with confectioners' sugar.

—CINDY PAWLYCN

LA PIGNA'S CHOCOLATE-ALMOND TORTE

There seems to be an endless number of desserts throughout Italy that use almonds. This one from La Pigna, in Capri, combines blanched almonds and chocolate for a rich, dense cake that develops a fuller flavor if made a day ahead. It is marvelous topped with a scoop of rich vanilla ice cream, or served on a pool of warm zabaglione.

SERVES 8

- 2 cups blanched whole almonds
- 6½ ounces unsweetened chocolate, coarsely chopped
- 7 large egg yolks
- 1 cup granulated sugar
- ¼ pound plus 5 tablespoons unsalted butter, at room temperature

  Confectioners' sugar, for dusting

1. Heat the oven to 350°. Butter the bottom of an 8-inch springform pan and line with a round of parchment or wax paper. Butter and flour the paper and the sides of the pan, and tap out the excess flour.

2. In a food processor or blender, combine the almonds and chocolate and pulse until ground medium-fine.

3. In a medium bowl, using an electric mixer, beat the egg yolks and sugar until pale yellow and fluffy. Add the butter and beat until smooth. Add the almond-chocolate mixture and beat until well blended, 2 to 3 minutes. The batter will be very dense. Scrape it into the prepared pan.

4. Bake the cake in the lower third of the oven until a toothpick stuck in the center comes out clean, about 45 minutes.

5. Let the cake cool in the pan for 5 minutes. Remove the sides of the pan and place the cake on a serving plate. Let cool completely. Just before serving, sift confectioners' sugar over the top.

—LA PIGNA, CAPRI, ITALY

WALNUT TORTE

This wonderful walnut pastry is from Aosta, capital city of the Valle d'Aosta, in northwestern Italy. The region is famous for its creamy butter and its walnuts. This version, also known as *torta di noci d'Aosta*, is inspired by the walnut torte at the Pasticceria Boch, one of the most elegant pastry shops in Northern Italy.

SERVES 8 TO 10

1¼ cups granulated sugar

½ teaspoon lemon juice

¾ cup light honey

½ pound plus 4 tablespoons unsalted butter, at room temperature

Pinch salt

2 cups coarsely chopped walnuts

3 large egg yolks

2 cups flour

Confectioners' sugar, for dusting

1. In a heavy medium saucepan, combine ½ cup of the granulated sugar with the lemon juice; stir well to mix. Cook over moderate heat, stirring occasionally, until the sugar melts and turns pale amber, 12 to 15 minutes. Stir in the honey and ¼ pound of the butter and bring to a boil over moderately high heat. Cool until thick bubbles form, 2 to 3 minutes. Stir in the salt and walnuts, remove from the heat, and let cool.

2. Heat the oven to 350°. Butter a 9-inch springform pan. In a large bowl, using an electric mixer, beat the remaining ¼ pound plus 4 tablespoons butter at high speed until smooth. Gradually beat in the remaining ¾ cup granulated sugar and beat until fluffy. Beat in the egg yolks one at a time. Using a rubber spatula, gradually mix in the flour until blended.

3. Divide the dough in half. With floured fingertips or knuckles, press half the dough evenly over the bottom and about 1 inch up the sides of the prepared pan. Spread the cooled nut filling evenly over the dough.

4. Sprinkle the remaining dough with flour and pat it into a 9-inch disk on a cardboard cake round or tart pan bottom; cover and refrigerate until well chilled.

5. Remove the dough from the cardboard or pan bottom and set over the filling in the pan. Press it into place, then crimp the edges with the tines of a fork to seal. Pierce the top in 10 to 12 places with the fork.

6. Bake the torte in the middle of the oven until lightly browned around the edges, 45 to 50 minutes. Let cool briefly in the pan, then unmold onto a rack to cool completely. Dust very lightly with confectioners' sugar before serving.

—NICK MALGIERI

ITALIAN CRUMB CAKE

This regional specialty comes from Treviso, a town near Venice. There are many versions, called *fregolatta*, (its name means "crumbly"); some are actually sponge cakes made with ground nuts. This very simple one is sort of a giant, buttery-rich crumbly cookie that's baked in a tart pan, cut into wedges, and served with coffee or tea.

SERVES 8

- 1 cup unblanched whole almonds
- 2½ cups flour
- 1 cup sugar
- ¼ teaspoon salt
- 2 teaspoons vanilla extract
- ½ pound unsalted butter, melted and cooled

1. Heat the oven to 350°. Butter a 10-inch tart pan with a removable bottom or a 9-inch pie pan.

2. Put the almonds in a food processor and pulse until coarsely ground; the pieces should be no larger than ⅛ inch.

3. In a medium bowl, whisk together the flour, sugar, and salt. Stir in the almonds.

4. Stir the vanilla into the melted butter and add to the dry ingredients. Stir with a rubber spatula until evenly combined. Rub the mixture between the palms of your hands to make crumbs no larger than ¼ inch.

5. Scatter three-quarters of the crumbs over the bottom of the prepared pan and press very lightly with your fingertips to compress. Scatter the remaining crumbs on top, but do not press them down. Bake in the middle of the oven until light golden and cooked through, about 25 minutes. Transfer to a rack to cool.

6. Remove the sides of the tart pan and slide the crumb cake off the pan bottom onto a platter before cutting into wedges, or serve directly from the pie pan.

—NICK MALGIERI

SAND TART

This subtle-tasting, delicate cake has an unusual but pleasantly grainy texture that results from the combination of fine-ground cornmeal and potato starch. It's related to a rich shortcake, but the baking powder and the beaten egg whites keep it light. Have a slice with a glass of dessert wine for a serene conclusion to your meal.

SERVES 6 TO 8

½ pound plus 2 tablespoons unsalted butter, at room temperature

1 cup fine white cornmeal

1 cup potato starch

1 tablespoon baking powder

½ teaspoon salt

1 cup plus 2 tablespoons granulated sugar

2 large eggs, separated

1 tablespoon anisette liqueur

½ teaspoon vanilla extract

Confectioners' sugar, for dusting

1. Heat the oven to 350°. Butter a 10-inch cake pan with 2 tablespoons of the butter.

2. In a medium bowl, whisk together the cornmeal, potato starch, baking powder, and salt. Set aside.

3. In another medium bowl, using an electric mixer, cream the granulated sugar and the remaining ½ pound butter until fluffy, 2 to 3 minutes. Beat in the egg yolks, anisette, and vanilla. Gradually beat in the cornmeal mixture; the batter will be dense.

4. In a medium bowl, beat the egg whites until they hold soft peaks when the beaters are lifted. Fold half the egg whites into the batter, then fold in the remaining whites. Scrape the batter into the prepared pan.

5. Bake the cake in the middle of the oven until a toothpick stuck in the center comes out clean, about 35 minutes. Transfer to a wire rack and let cool completely.

6. Dust the top of the cake with confectioners' sugar. Because this is such a delicate cake, it's best to serve it directly from the pan. Cut with a sharp knife and carefully remove the pieces with a cake server.

—TOM MARESCA AND DIANE DARROW

PEACH AND RAISIN RISOTTO

The short-grain arborio rice that makes creamy risotto can also be turned into a sweet rice pudding. The technique is similar to that used for traditionally made risotto, but instead of gradually stirring hot broth into the rice, use a simple sugar syrup. Enriched with currants, peaches, and a splash of dark rum, this warm risotto makes a comforting cold-weather dessert.

SERVES 4 TO 6

2   10-ounce packages frozen peaches in syrup, thawed

4   tablespoons unsalted butter

½   cup currants

1   cup arborio rice

2   tablespoons dark rum

2   tablespoons granulated sugar

½   cup heavy cream

     Brown sugar, for serving

1. Drain the peaches, reserving the syrup. Cut the peaches into ½-inch pieces.

2. In a medium saucepan, combine the syrup with enough water to measure 4 cups. Bring to a simmer.

3. In a large heavy saucepan, melt 2 tablespoons of the butter over moderate heat. Add the currants and cook for 2 minutes. Add the rice and stir until well coated with the butter and slightly translucent, 1 to 2 minutes. Add the rum and cook, stirring, until it has been absorbed.

4. Add ½ cup of the simmering syrup and cook, stirring constantly, until the syrup has been almost completely absorbed. The rice and liquid should bubble gently; adjust the heat as needed. Continue cooking and stirring the rice, adding the syrup ½ cup at a time and allowing the rice to absorb the liquid before adding the next ½ cup. Cook until the rice is almost tender but still slightly crunchy in the center, 20 to 25 minutes.

5. Add the granulated sugar, peaches, and cream. Continue to cook, stirring and adding syrup ¼ cup at a time as necessary, until the rice is tender but still firm, 3 to 6 minutes longer.

6. Stir in the remaining 2 tablespoons butter. Serve with a bowl of brown sugar.

VANILLA-WALNUT COOKIES

The Italian name for these crisp, thin cookies, *brutti ma buone*, translates as "ugly but good." Their appearance may leave something to be desired, but they are delicious eaten with milk, and they make a fine accompaniment to vanilla ice cream. Do not be deterred by the large amount of vanilla extract.

MAKES ABOUT 2 DOZEN

1 cup sifted flour

½ cup sugar

½ cup chopped walnuts

¼ pound unsalted butter, at room temperature

½ teaspoon salt

2 tablespoons vanilla extract

3 large eggs

1. Heat the oven to 350°. Lightly grease two large baking sheets.

2. In a medium bowl, whisk together the flour, sugar, and walnuts.

3. In another medium bowl, with an electric mixer, beat the butter until fluffy. Beat in the salt and vanilla. Beat in the eggs one at a time.

4. On low speed, beat in half of the flour mixture until just blended. Beat in the remaining flour mixture just until smooth.

5. Drop a rounded tablespoon of dough onto a prepared baking sheet. With the back of a spoon, spread the dough out to a thin round about 3 inches in diameter. Continue until you have filled both baking sheets. Cover and refrigerate the remaining dough.

6. Bake the cookies until they are browned at the edges and light golden in the middle, 18 to 20 minutes. Transfer to wire racks to cool. Repeat with the remaining cookie dough, allowing the baking sheets to cool before starting the next batch.

—FRANK CALDWELL

ITALIAN COOKIES

Cookies have always been a part of Italian eating. Italians enjoy them for breakfast, as a mid-morning snack with a cup of espresso, at the conclusion of a midday or evening meal, at teatime, and dunked into a glass of *vin santo* at the end of the day.

Every region or town has its own local cookie. Saronna is famous for its *amaretti* and Sicily for its *pignolate*. There are also *ricciarelli* from Siena, *baca di dama* (lady's kisses) from Piedmont, *brutti ma buone* from Florence, and *marasche* from Bologna.

CORNMEAL CRESCENT BISCOTTI

These cookies, *crumiri*, come from Piedmont, where cornmeal is often turned into polenta. These biscotti are very delicate and particularly well suited to pairing with light sparkling wines. Unlike denser biscotti, they require only a quick dip in the wine rather than a heavy dunking.

MAKES ABOUT 4 DOZEN

1¾ cups flour

¾ cup fine yellow cornmeal

1 teaspoon salt

½ pound unsalted butter, at room temperature

¾ cup sugar

1 large egg

1 teaspoon vanilla extract

1. In a medium bowl, whisk together the flour, cornmeal, and salt.

2. In a large bowl, using an electric mixer, cream the butter and sugar until fluffy. Beat in the egg and vanilla. Stir in the dry ingredients until well blended. Cover and refrigerate the dough until firm enough to handle, at least 1 hour.

3. Heat the oven to 375°. Butter and flour two large baking sheets.

4. Scoop up 1 heaping tablespoon of the dough and roll into a log about 2 inches long. Bend to form a crescent shape and put on a prepared baking sheet. Repeat with the remaining dough, placing the biscotti about 2 inches apart on the baking sheets. With your hands or the back of a wooden spoon, lightly flatten the biscotti.

5. Bake the biscotti until golden brown, 15 to 20 minutes. Transfer to wire racks to cool.

—MICHELE SCICOLONE

CHOCOLATE-WALNUT BISCOTTI

Biscotti di ciocolata are sometimes called *mostaccioli* because of their mustache shape. These nut-studded cookies are dry, crunchy, and hard because they are baked not once, but twice. They will soften up immediately when dipped into a glass of *vin santo*, the sweet Italian dessert wine, or port.

MAKES ABOUT 4 DOZEN

- 2 cups walnut halves
- 3 ounces unsweetened chocolate
- 5 tablespoons plus 1 teaspoon unsalted butter
- 2 cups flour
- 2 teaspoons baking powder
- 3 large eggs
- 1 cup sugar
- 1 teaspoon grated orange zest

1. Heat the oven to 350°. Put the walnuts on a baking sheet and toast in the oven until golden brown, about 10 minutes. Let cool and coarsely chop.

2. In a double boiler over simmering water, melt the chocolate with butter, stirring until smooth. Let cool for 10 minutes.

3. In a medium bowl, whisk together the flour and baking powder.

4. In a large bowl, beat the eggs lightly. Gradually beat in the sugar. Beat in the orange zest. Stir in the cooled chocolate. Stir in the dry ingredients until blended.

Fold in the walnuts. Divide the dough in half, wrap in plastic, and refrigerate for at least 1 hour, or overnight.

5. Heat the oven to 350°. Butter a large baking sheet. Shape each half of dough into a 14 by 2½-inch log. Put the logs about 4 inches apart on the baking sheet. Smooth the tops and sides with a rubber spatula. Bake in the middle of the oven until the logs are firm when pressed in the center, 40 to 45 minutes. Remove the baking sheet from the oven; do not turn off the oven.

6. Carefully slide the logs onto a cutting board. Using a serrated knife, cut each log diagonally into ½-inch slices. Arrange the slices, upright on edge, on the baking sheet and bake until crisp, about 15 minutes longer. Transfer to wire racks to cool completely.

—MICHELE SCICOLONE

Hazelnut Biscotti with Black Pepper

Adding black pepper to biscotti is quite common in Italy. In fact, the pepper biscotti called *taralli* are found everywhere and in many varieties. The combination of black pepper and hazelnuts makes a satisfying biscotti, especially if served with a glass of sweet wine for dipping.

MAKES ABOUT 2 DOZEN

1½   cups hazelnuts

1¾   cups flour

½   teaspoon baking soda

½   teaspoon baking powder

⅛   teaspoon salt

1½   teaspoons fresh-ground black pepper

¼   pound unsalted butter, at room temperature

1   cup sugar

2   large eggs

1   teaspoon grated lemon zest

1   teaspoon grated orange zest

1½   teaspoons vanilla extract

¼   teaspoon almond extract

1. Heat the oven to 350°. Put the hazelnuts on a baking sheet and toast in the oven until the skins crack and loosen and the nuts are golden brown, about 15 minutes. Wrap the warm nuts in a kitchen towel and rub them together to remove most of the skins. Coarsely chop.

2. In a medium bowl, whisk together the flour, baking soda, baking powder, salt, and pepper.

3. In a large bowl, using an electric mixer, beat the butter and sugar on medium speed until fluffy, about 3 minutes. Beat in the eggs one at a time. Beat in the lemon and orange zests, the vanilla, and almond extract. Fold in the hazelnuts and the dry ingredients just until incorporated.

4. Butter a large baking sheet. Divide the dough in half. Shape each half into a 12-inch log, 3 inches wide and 1 inch high. Put the logs about 4 inches apart on the prepared baking sheet. Bake in the middle of the oven until the logs are lightly browned and firm when pressed in the center, about 25 minutes. Let cool on the baking sheet for about 10 minutes; do not turn off the oven.

5. Carefully slide the logs onto a cutting board. Using a serrated knife, cut them into ¾-inch slices. Arrange the slices, cut-side down, on the baking sheet and bake until golden brown, 15 minutes longer. Transfer to a rack and let cool completely.

—Evan Kleiman

CHESTNUT-FLOUR FRITTERS

These light, sweet fritters once were among the most common of all preparations made with chestnut flour. The batter is thin and it is meant to be. It is best to eat these fritters as soon as they are made. Light-brown chestnut flour is imported from Italy, where it is milled in the fall and winter when the chestnuts are harvested. It is available at Italian specialty food markets.

MAKES ABOUT 18

1 cup chestnut flour, sifted

¾ cup milk

1 tablespoon sugar, plus more for sprinkling

Pinch salt

1½ tablespoons raisins

4 cups vegetable oil

1. Put the chestnut flour in a medium bowl and make a well in the center. Gradually add the milk, stirring constantly with a wooden spoon to prevent lumps. When the batter is smooth, stir in the sugar, salt, and raisins.

2. In a large deep frying pan or deep fryer, heat the oil over moderate heat to 375°. Carefully add the batter by tablespoonfuls, leaving space to allow for spreading. Fry, turning, until evenly browned, about 2 minutes. Using a slotted spoon, transfer the fritters to a paper-towel-lined platter to drain. Repeat with the remaining batter.

3. Remove the paper towels from the platter, sprinkle the fritters with sugar, and serve immediately.

—GIULIANO BUGIALLI

DESSERT WINES

Italians are fond of serving dry cakes and cookies that are destined to be served with (and often dipped in) a dessert wine. Here are a number of options worth sampling:

• Asti Spumante: A sparkling wine from Piedmont made from the muscat grape.

• Moscato d'Asti: The less-sparkling version of Asti Spumante.

• Malvasia delle Lipari: Made from the malvasia grape; produced on several small islands of the coast of Sicily.

• Marsala Vergine: A fortified wine from Sicily.

• Picolit: A relatively rare dessert wine from Friuli-Venezia Giulia; made from the picolit grape.

• Vin Santo: The classic biscotti-dipping wine; made all over Italy, but the best comes from Tuscany.

Opposite: Marinated Cucumbers (top), page 231, and Chestnut-Flour Fritters

MENUS

Italian-Style Brunch

Bellinis

Assorted Olives

Rosemary Grissini, page 211

———

Pasta Frittata, page 183

Fried Zucchini, page 254

Champagne

———

Walnut Torte, page 279

Cappuccino

Spring Dinner

Scallops Venetian-Style, page 64

Gradnik Sauvignon Blanc
or *Bollini Pinot Grigio*

———

Rice with Peas, page 68

———

Hotel Palumbo's
Baked Striped Bass, page 178

Baked Fennel with Parmesan, page 234

Fiano di Avellino

———

Strawberries with Lemon and Sugar

Coffee Semifreddo, page 266

Vanilla-Walnut Cookies, page 285

Espresso

Italian Dinner

Grilled Prosciutto and Fontina
Cheese Panini, page 37

———

Zucchini and Arborio Rice Soup,
page 48

———

Lamb Chops Milanese, page 150

Asparagus with Brown Butter and
Parmesan, page 224

Chianti Classico

———

Bitter Greens Tossed with Fruity
Olive Oil, Coarse Salt, and Garlic

———

Italian Cheeses

Chocolate and Pistachio Cannoli,
page 276

Casual Spring Dinner

Artichokes with Garlic and Fresh Mint,
page 59

———

Roast Leg of Lamb
with Mustard Coating, page 148

Olive Bread, page 209

Asparagus with Brown Butter
and Parmesan, page 224

Chianti Classico

———

Melon Sorbet with Port, page 262

Castellare Grappa

Dinner al Fresco

Kirs

Homemade Herbed Ricotta Cheese,
page 25

Mixed Olives

———

Bow Ties with Veal, Lemon,
and Pine Nut Sauce, page 105

Italian Herbed Bread Toasts

Chianti or *Rosso di Montalcino*

———

Radicchio and Endive Salad

———

Peach and Raisin Risotto,

page 284

Espresso

Light Summer
Lunch

*Sweet Vermouth on the Rocks with
Lemon Twists*

Sweet-and-Hot Melon, page 17

———

Pasta with Fresh Tuna, page 93

Sangiovese

———

Chicory, Romaine, and Onion Salad

———

Ricotta Gelato, page 263

Iced Cappuccino

Columbus Day Lunch

Sweet Vermouth on the Rocks

Herbed Mozzarella, page 26

————

Artichoke, Chickpea, and Fennel Giambotta with Chicken, page 164

Rosemary Focaccia, page 205

Orvieto

————

Salad of Bitter Greens

————

Chocolate and Pistachio Cannoli, page 276

Espresso

Simple Tuscan Supper

Figs Agrodolce, page 24

Tuscan Beans with Tuna, Pancetta, and Lemon, page 181

Green Salad with Walnut Oil Vinaigrette

Pinot Bianco or *Pinot Grigio*

————

Assorted Cheeses and Fruits

Marinated Cucumbers, page 231

Melon Sorbet with Port, page 262

Backyard
Picnic

Wine Spritzers

Olive-Stuffed Pepper Wedges with
Tomatoes and Anchovies, page 21

———

Mushroom and Mozzarella Sandwiches,
page 214

Pasta Salad with Broccoli
and Tuna, page 97

Tocai Friulano

———

Strawberry Granita

Italian Crumb Cake, page 280

End-of-Summer
Dinner Party

Vodka Tonics

Frittata Wedges, page 28

Red-Wine-Marinated Shallots, page 18

———

Capellini with Calamari
and Shrimp, page 98

———

Vitello Tonnato, page 136

Zucchini with Fresh Thyme, page 255

Bardolino

———

Tomato and Arugula Salad with
Ricotta Salata and Lemon Dressing

———

Tiramisu, page 269

Espresso

Easy Sunday Supper

Mussels Marinara, page 65

Lacryma Christi

——

Sage-and-Pepper-Rubbed
Veal Roast, page 135

Broccoli Rabe with
Orecchiette, page 229

Dolcetto

——

Ricotta Gelato, page 263

Coffee

Autumn Dinner

Wild Mushroom Crostini, page 39

Pio Cesare Barbera

——

Sautéed Calf's Liver and
Onions, page 147

Pan-Grilled Radicchio with
Anchovy-Mustard Sauce, page 248

Amarone della Valpolicella

——

Sand Tart, page 283

A Supper for Friends

Open Bar

Assorted Antipasti

———

Baked Rigatoni with Braised Beef,
Olives, and Mozzarella, page 116

Tuscan Bread, page 212

Barolo

———

Spinach, Radicchio, and Chicory Salad
with Vinaigrette

———

Chestnut-Flour Fritters, page 290

Coffee

Campanian-Style Dinner

Spaghettini with Uncooked Tomato and
Black Olive Sauce, page 82

———

Veal Scaloppine Capannina, page 137

Herbed Carrots and Green Beans,
page 240

Friuli Cabernet

———

Arugula and Basil Salad with Oil and
Tarragon Vinegar

———

Molded Ricotta and Mascarpone with
Strawberries, page 272

Festa Italiana

Negronis

Assorted Antipasti

———

Potato Gnocchi with Tomato Sauce,
page 107

———

Roasted Herb-Stuffed Snapper with
Eggplant-Tomato Compote, page 176

Herbed Skillet Flatbread, page 206

Dolcetto

———

Italian Greens with Tomatoes

———

Sicilian Ricotta Cheesecake, page 275

Fruit

Espresso

Fall Supper

Campari and Sodas

Rosemary-and-Orange
Roasted Peppers, page 14

———

Carpaccio with Parmesan Shavings,
page 35

———

Giambotta of Mixed Greens with
Spareribs, page 156

Sage and Walnut Corn Cakes, page 213

Barbera

———

Chocolate-Walnut Biscotti, page 287

Espresso

Amaretto

Fireside Dinner

Ossobuco with Gremolata, page 133

Risotto alla Milanese, page 71

Green Beans with Olive Oil
and Garlic, page 237

Vino Nobile di Montepulciano

———

Sand Tart, page 283

Vietti Moscato

Cozy Italian Supper

White Wine Spritzers

Parmesan Crostini, page 38

———

Marinated Mushrooms with Roasted Red
Peppers and Arugula, page 16

———

Lasagne with Roast Chicken and Porcini
Mushrooms, page 110

Chianti Classico Riserva

———

Espresso Granita, page 267

Italian Crumb Cake, page 280

Coffee

Sit-Down Dinner with Friends

Mussels with Herbed Crumb
Topping, page 66

———

Olive and Roasted Red Pepper
Pizza, page 192

Vernaccia di San Gimignano

———

Pork Medallions with Arugula and
Tomatoes, page 160

Valpolicella

———

Italian Cheeses

Cornmeal Crescent Biscotti, page 286

Raisins Soaked in Grappa, page 261

Tuscan Feast

Wild Mushroom Crostini, page 39

———

Ligurian Vegetable Soup, page 47

———

Tuscan Roast Loin of Pork, page 155

Roasted Eggplant with Arugula, page 232

Barbaresco

———

Oranges with Sweet Basil
Zabaglione, page 270

Vin Santo

Roman Buffet

Campari and Sodas

Assorted Antipasti

———

Garlic-Shrimp Risotto, page 74

Verdicchio

———

Beef Tenderloin with Juniper, page 144

Green Beans with Balsamic-Glazed
Onions, page 238

Dolcetto d'Alba

———

Caprella, Gorgonzola, and
Bel Paese Cheeses

Rosemary Grissini, page 211

———

Green Grapes and Pears

La Pigna's Chocolate-Almond
Torte, page 278

Espresso

Sambuca con Mosca

A Grand Buffet

Pancetta-Wrapped Scallops with
Lemons, page 34

Carpaccio with Parmesan Shavings,
page 35

Tomato-Basil Crostini, page 40

Dolcetto

———

Veal Rolls with Peas, page 142

Chicken Breasts with Fennel Sauce,
page 162

Baked Risotto with Prosciutto,
page 73

Spinach with Raisins and Pine Nuts,
page 250

Roasted Asparagus, page 225

Pinot Bianco

———

Mascarpone Cream Dessert, page 274

Strawberry Sherbet with Cherry-Caramel
Sauce, page 264

Raisins Soaked in Grappa, page 261

Hearty Buffet

Puccinis

Garlic Bread with Prosciutto di Parma

Figs Agrodolce, page 24

Artichokes with Garlic and
Fresh Mint, page 59

Rosemary-and-Orange Roasted
Peppers, page 14

———

Penne with Lamb Ragu, page 102

Country-Style Fried Chicken, page 166

Spinach and Roasted Red Pepper Gratin,
page 249

Fall Vegetable Spiedini, page 253

Brunello di Montalcino or
Italian Chardonnay

———

Salad of Mixed Greens and
Fennel with Vinaigrette

———

Pears, Peaches, and Grapes

Tiramisu, page 269

Cornmeal Crescent Biscotti, page 286

INDEX

Page numbers in **boldface** indicate photographs

W

Z

CONTRIBUTORS

Katherine Alford is a food writer and cooking instructor in New York City.

Nancy Verde Barr is a food writer, cooking teacher, and the author of *We Called It Macaroni* (Knopf).

Brigit Legere Binns is a food writer. Her first book, *Polenta* (Chronicle Books), will be published spring 1997.

Giuliano Bugialli is a cooking teacher in New York City and Florence, Italy, and the author of *The Fine Art of Italian Cooking* (2nd edition, Times Books/Random House), *Giuliano Bugialli's Classic Techniques of Italian Cooking* (Simon and Schuster), *Giuliano Bugialli's Foods of Italy* (Stewart, Tabori & Chang), and *Bugialli on Pasta* (Simon and Schuster).

Anna Teresa Callen is a food writer, cooking teacher (Anna Teresa Callen Italian Cooking School, New York City), and the author of *Menus for Pasta* and *The Wonderful World of Pizzas, Quiches and Savory Pies* (both from Crown).

Kevin Cauldwell is the pastry chef at San Domenico in New York City.

Bob Chambers is the executive chef for Lancôme/L'Oreal Inc. He is also a food writer and food stylist.

Mark Cox was formerly the chef at Tony's in Houston.

Peggy Cullen is a baker, candy maker, and food writer who lives in New York City.

Diane Darrow is a food writer and co-author with her husband, Tom Maresca, of two books on Italian food and wine. A number of their recipes that appear in this book are from *La Tavola Italiana* (William Morrow) and *The Seasons of the Italian Kitchen* (Atlantic Monthly Press).

Julia della Croce is a foodwriter and teacher. She is the author of *Pasta Classica: The Art of Italian Pasta Cooking*, *The Pasta Book: Recipes in the Italian Tradition*, and her most recent, *Antipasti: The Little Dishes of Italy* (all from Chronicle Books).

Constance and Rosario Del Nero are co-authors of *Risotto: A Taste of Milan* (Harper & Row). Constance is a cookbook illustrator and freelance writer. Rosario is a Corporate Chef for Bertucci's, a chain of brick-oven Italian restaurants located principally in the northeast. He also teaches regional French and Italian cooking at The Cambridge School of Culinary Arts in Cambridge, Massachusetts.

Lorenza de'Medici is a food writer, cooking teacher (The Villa Table, Siena, Italy), and the author of a number of books, including *Italy the Beautiful Cookbook* (Collins), *The Renaissance of Italian Cooking* (Fawcett Columbine), and *The Heritage of Italian Cooking* (Random House).

Anne Disrude is a New York-based food stylist.

Georgia Chan Downard is a cookbook author, food stylist, and cooking teacher in New York City.

Bette Duke is a New York-based designer.

Mary Ewing-Mulligan, responsible for the wine recommendations in this book, is the only American woman who is a Master of Wine. She is co-owner and director of the International Wine Center in New York and has co-authored such books as *Wine for Dummies*, *White Wine for Dummies*, and *Red Wine for Dummies* (all from IDG Books). She is currently the wine columnist of *The Daily News* and contributes to several publications including *Martha Stewart Living* and the *Wine Enthusiast*.

Fred Ferretti is the author of *Gourmet* magazine's monthly column "A Gourmet at Large."

Carol Field is a food writer and the author of *The Italian Baker* (HarperCollins), *Celebrating Italy* (William Morrow), *Italy in Small Bites* (William Morrow), *Focaccia* (Chronicle Books), and *In Nonna's Kitchen* (HarperCollins).

Jim Flint is an avid home cook specializing in Italian cuisine.

Jim Fobel, a James Beard Foundation Award Winner for *Jim Fobel's Big Flavors*, was formerly the director of *Food & Wine* magazine's test kitchen and is the author of eight books, including *Jim Fobel's Casseroles* (Clarkson Potter), *Jim Fobel's Diet Feasts* (Doubleday), and *Jim Fobel's Old-Fashioned Baking Book* (Ballantine).

Sarah Fritschner is the author of *Express Lane Cookbook* and *Vegetarian Express Lane Cookbook* (both from Chapters) and is the food editor of the *Courier-Journal* in Louisville, Kentucky. She is also a public speaker on food and nutrition issues and makes regular television appearances.

George Germon and Johanne Killeen are chefs and co-owners of Al Forno in Providence, Rhode Island, and the author of *Cucina Simpatica* (HarperCollins).

Edward Giobbi is a painter-sculptor and the author of *Italian Family Cooking* (Random House), *Eat Right Eat Well—The Italian Way*, and *Pleasures of the Good Earth* (both from Knopf).

Susan Shapiro Jaslove is a food writer and recipe developer.

Stephen Kalt is a restaurant consultant and chef/co-owner of Spartina in New York City.

Marcia Kiesel is the associate director of *Food & Wine* magazine's test kitchen and co-author of *Simple Art of Vietnamese Cooking* (Prentice Hall).

Evan Kleiman is the chef/owner of Angeli Caffe on Melrose in Los Angeles. She is the author of *Cucina del Mare* (William Morrow) as well as the co-author, with Viana La Place, of *Cucina Fresca* (Harper & Row), *Cucina Rustica*, and *Pasta Fresca* (both from William Morrow).

Viana La Place is a food writer, cooking teacher, and author of *Verdura, Vegetables Italian Style* (William Morrow). She is also co-author, with Evan Kleiman, of *Cucina Rustica, Pasta Fresca* (both from William Morrow), and *Cucina Fresca* (Harper & Row).

Stephanie Lyness is a food writer and recipe developer. She is the translator of Jacques Manière's cookbook, *Cuisine à la Vapeur: The Art of Cooking with Steam* (William Morrow) and has just completed *Cooking with Steam* (William Morrow).

Deborah Madison is a cooking teacher as well as a former chef and restaurateur. She is the author of *The Greens Cookbook* and *The Savory Way* (both from Bantam) and *The Vegetarian Taste* (Chronicle Books). She is working on a vegetarian cookbook.

Nicky Major is the owner of the catering firm Major the Gourmet and the restaurant MTG Cafe to Go in Vancouver, British Columbia.

Nick Malgieri is the director of the baking program at Peter Kump's New York Cooking School and is the author of *Nick Malgieri's Perfect Pastry* (Macmillan) and *Great Italian Desserts* (Little, Brown).

Tony Mantuano is chef/owner of Mangia and Tuttaposto, both in Kenosha, Wisconsin.

Tom Maresca is a food and wine writer and author of *Mastering Wine* and *The Right Wine* (both Grove Press). He is also co-author with his wife, Diane Darrow, of two books on Italian food and wine. A number of their recipes that appear in this book are from *La Tavola Italiana* (William Morrow) and *The Seasons of the Italian Kitchen* (Atlantic Monthly Press).

Zarela Martinez is the chef/owner of Zarela in New York City.

John Robert Massie is a New York-based food stylist.

Michael McLaughlin is a co-author, with Sheila Lukins and Julee Rosso, of *The Silver Palate Cookbook* (Workman) and the author of several books, among them *The Manhattan Chili Company Southwest American Cookbook* (Crown), *Weekends in the New American Kitchen*, *Fifty-Two Meatloaves* (all from Simon and Schuster), and most recently *The Little Book of Big Sandwiches* and *Good Mornings* (both from Chronicle).

Mark Militello is chef/owner of Mark's Place in North Miami, Florida.

Grace Parisi is a chef, food writer, and food stylist. Her new book, *Summer/Winter Pasta* (Quill) is due out in 1997.

Cindy Pawlcyn is chef of Mustard's in St. Helena, California.

W. Peter Prestcott is Entertaining & Special Projects Editor of *Food & Wine* magazine.

Carl Quagliata is chef at Giovanni's Ristorante in Beachwood, Ohio.

Alvio Renzini is a professor at the University of Bologna and an avid Italian cook.

Michael Rich, an astronomer by day, is an enthusiastic cook in his off hours.

Margaret and G. Franco Romagnoli are food writers, TV chefs, and the authors of *The New Romagnolis' Table, New Italian Cooking, Carnevale Italiano, The Romagnolis' Table* (all from Atlantic/Little, Brown), *The Italian Fish Cookbook* and *Zuppa!* (both from Henry Holt and Co.).

Richard Sax was the author of several books, among them *Classic Home Desserts* (Chapters) and *Get in There and Cook* (Clarkson Potter), due out in 1997.

Michele Scicolone is a food and wine writer and the author of *A Fresh Taste of Italy* (Broadway Books), and *The Antipasto Table* and *La Dolce Vita* (both from William Morrow). She teaches Italian cooking classes at schools around the country.

Tracy Seaman is the Test Kitchen Director for *Great American Home Cooking*. She is also the author of several cookbooks.

Martha Rose Shulman is the author of eleven cookbooks, her most recent, *Great Breads* (Chapters Publishing), explores home-baked favorites from Europe, The British Isles, and North America.

Steven Singer is Corporate Executive Chef of the Sfuzzi restaurants.

Rick Spinell is the chef/owner of Spinell's Litchfield Food Company in Litchfield, Connecticut.

Diana Sturgis is director of *Food & Wine* magazine's test kitchen.

Jean-Georges Vongerichten is the chef/owner of three restaurants, Vong, Jo Jo, and Lipstick Cafe, all in New York City. He is the author of *Simple Cuisine* (Simon and Schuster) and is working on a new cookbook on Thai cuisine.

Ari Weinzweig is the co-owner of Zingerman's Delicatessen, Markadia (a specialty produce market), and Zingerman's Bakehouse, all in Ann Arbor, Michigan.

Patricia Wells is the restaurant critic for *The International Herald Tribune* in Paris and the author of numerous cookbooks, including *Bistro Cooking, The Food Lover's Guide to France, The Food Lover's Guide to Paris* (all from Workman), *Simply Fresh, Patricia Wells' Trattoria* (both from William Morrow), and the forthcoming *At Home with Patricia Wells* (Scribner).

We would also like to thank the following individuals and restaurants for their contributions to *Food & Wine* magazine and to this cookbook:

Amerigo's, The Bronx, New York; Capers Catering, Chicago; Cibreo, Florence, Italy; Da Celestino, Florence, Italy; Donatello, San Francisco; Enoteca Pinchiorri, Florence, Italy; Hotel Palumbo, Ravello, Italy; La Campana, Rome, Italy; La Capannina, Capri, Italy; La Pigna, Capri, Italy; Sambuco, Porto Garibaldi, Italy; Spiaggia, Chicago; Tony's, Houston; Rick Tramonto and Gale Gand, Trio, Evanston, Illinois; Trattoria Pasqualino, Rome, Italy.

PHOTOGRAPHY CREDITS

Cover Photo: Steven Mark Needham (Spaghettini with Uncooked Tomato and Black Olive Sauce, page 83).

Back Photos: Steven Mark Needham (Ossobuco with Gremolata, page 132; Insalata di Mare, page 32; Ligurian Vegetable Soup, page 46; Grilled Prosciutto and Fontina Cheese Panini, page 36; Green Beans with Balsamic-Glazed Onions, page 239; Hazelnut Biscotti with Black Pepper, page 289).

David Bishop: 291, 141; **Dennis Galante:** 207; **Maria Robledo:** 281; **Jerry Simpson:** 2, 87, 197, 198, 273, 277; **Mark Thomas:** 41, 42, 72, 88, 111, 146, 260, 265, 282; **Elizabeth Watt:** 114, 119; All other photographs by **Steven Mark Needham**.

Food Styling: Grady Best and Anne Disrude
Prop Styling: Adrienne Abseck